STOP LISTENING

A Young Professional's Journey to Leading in Business, Building Wealth, and Ignoring the Haters

MATTHEW BILLS

LITERARY CURRENCY
PUBLISHING CO.

LITERARY CURRENCY
PUBLISHING CO.

STOP LISTENING. © 2019 by Matthew Bills. All rights reserved. Printed in the United States of America. No part of this book may be used or reproduced in any manner whatsoever without written permission except in the case of brief quotations embodied in critical articles and reviews.

FIRST EDITION

Cover Art by Michael Bills. Thanks, brother!
Business Inquiries: www.michaelbills.com

ISBN 978-0-9600637-0-3

To my parents, Michael and Megan Bills, for the example you set, encouragement you bestowed, and your selfless, unwavering service to our country.

"WITHOUT HUSTLE, TALENT WILL ONLY CARRY YOU SO FAR."

— Gary Vaynerchuk

Contents

Introduction

Chapter 1: Choose Your Priorities & Change Your Life
    Clear Your Runway

Chapter 2: Nice to Meet You
    I Am Not Special
    Privilege

Chapter 3: Life as an Army Brat
    The Duffel Bag
    Life Lessons from Skateboarding

Chapter 4: What They Don't Teach You in High School
    High School Does Not Define You
    Experience Matters
    What You Should Have Been Taught
    Your Parents are Not Your Piggy Bank
    Let's Talk About College

Chapter 5: Be a Grown Ass Person
    Put in the Time – Your Personal Brand Will Thank You
    Four Toxic Words: That's Not My Job
    Four A.M. Warehouse
    Entitled to What?
    Trophies

Chapter 6: Dollars and Sense
    Building Wealth
    Philosophy of Saving and Risk Tolerance
    Start Young
    Credit Cards and Building Credit
    Don't Have It? Don't Spend It!

Chapter 7: Leading in Business
    Own Your Destiny

    The Bike Before the Benz
    Dress the Part
    Emotional Intelligence
    Success Doesn't Happen Alone
    Rise to the Challenge
    Some Days Suck
    Sometimes You Have to Laugh

Chapter 8: Power of the Side Hustle
    Just Google It
    Invest in Yourself
    Real Estate

Chapter 9: Do People Hate You? Good!
    Kids. My Choice. Not Yours
    Keyboard Warriors
    Luck, Huh?
    Check Yourself
    Success Guilt
    Giving Back

Chapter 10: My Silent Enemy
    Anxiety
    A State of Ignorance
    Anxiety Knows No Age Boundaries
    Perspective

Chapter 11: The Money Mindset
    There's Enough to Go Around
    Money Doesn't Remove Passion
    Are You Willing?

Chapter 12: Time to Choose

Acknowledgments
About the Author
References

Introduction

We live in a time of unprecedented access. Access to information, to tools, and to people. This raging river of data has armed us with the ability to propel our society forward at a pace that is intriguingly challenging to keep up with. We live in a time when an individual can create and launch a business from his or her phone. We live in a time when million-dollar deals can be made over a text message and partnerships are formed in a matter of seconds with someone on the other side of the world. It truly is an incredible time to be alive! However, that unfiltered rush of information and opportunity poses a challenge. How does one navigate the static and tune to their desired channel? How does one leverage these resources to build and live an extraordinary life?

Each day, countless individuals fail to take their lives into their own hands. Their decisions feed a vicious cycle of financial strain, career stagnation, and a perpetually growing belief that one's failure to achieve success is somehow the fault of everyone except the person in the mirror. These unfavorable trends are more preventable than most care to recognize, but so few choose to put in the time and work needed to drastically change the outlook of their life and the lives of generations to come. I am writing this book because of two very simple reasons:

1. I want you to stop listening to the traditional guidance and social conventions that plague the minds of our society.

2. I want to see you win.

This is not a typical self-help book or financial planning book. This book is written with an autobiographical flare, providing insight to some often-comical experiences I had at a young age—not only to leave you laughing, but also to emphasize I am not special, and you, too, *can* achieve your desired level of success.

You have already made a great decision by picking up this book. Read it. Take note of which aspects speak to you. Whether you are in high school or twenty years into your career, push yourself to put aside the traditional guidance you have received. Learn from my personal experiences, and think about how you can apply them to change your position in life. The experiences, and more importantly the results, I describe are as real as the air you and I breathe. There is no reason why you cannot achieve every bit of professional and financial success that you desire. Follow me on this journey to leading in business, building wealth, and ignoring the haters.

Matthew Bills
Corporate Leader, Author and Entrepreneur

Chapter 1: Choose Your Priorities and Change Your Life

Over the last decade, one constant characteristic I've observed in people who are failing to get ahead in life is that their priorities are, to put it bluntly, complete shit. As you'll hear me say multiple times throughout this book, I don't spend much, if any, of my time worrying about what other people are doing. This is mainly because I'm focused on my own priorities and how I can be of value to others. However, how often do you hear a family member, friend or acquaintance complaining about their circumstances, only to be followed up by actions, or lack thereof, that further back them into an unfavorable corner? Unfavorable actions such as living beyond their means, racking up credit card debt, not doing what they need to do to get ahead at work, blaming others for their shortcomings and so forth.

Much of my success, financially or otherwise, has been directly related to knowing, owning, and living my priorities. What's interesting is that my priorities haven't changed since I was eighteen years old. Whether it was when my wife and I had a household income of $50K or over $500k, our core priorities did not waver. Our core priorities centered around saving money, advancing in our careers, and setting ourselves up to build wealth.

I graduated high school in 2006 and at the time of writing this book, I am thirty-one years old. I serve as Director of Client Services at a leading payments company and lead a team of Fraud Strategists. While employed with my previous employer, TSYS Merchant Solutions, I became one of the youngest individuals in the company's over thirty-five-year history to be promoted to Associate Director at age twenty-five, followed by Director at twenty-seven. The right priorities, my friends, is how I made this happen.

For example, when my wife and I were finishing high school, we both knew that our respective career paths at the time would require some form of higher education. We knew that, like so many people, if we didn't tackle college right away, with every passing year it would become more and more difficult to go back to school. So, straight out of high school, college success was our priority.

Perhaps the scenario of a college education isn't applicable to you. Regardless, it is a great example of how my wife and I chose our priorities, stuck with them, and did not waver.

This same level of dedication can be applied to any aspect of your life. Stop listening to what society tells you should be a priority and, instead, make your priorities align with what is important to you and what makes you happy in life. I don't care if you're nineteen or fifty, what you are choosing to make a priority does not need to align with societal norms. The number of times Kim and I were told that what we were focusing on at ages eighteen, twenty-two, twenty-seven, and so on was silly, is insane.

"Why would you worry about investing money when you're nineteen?"

"Why do you have a last will and testament at such a young age?"

"Why do you make your career such a priority at such a young age?"

"Don't you know you have plenty of time to worry about saving money?"

The list goes on and on. As you read this book, I challenge you to take a few moments to identify your priorities. Have you been living your priorities? What is standing in your way? Know them, own them, and allow them to shape your life.

Clear Your Runway

There you are, a skilled pilot, sitting in the cockpit of the airplane. You have clearance from the tower to take off. Your sole responsibility as the pilot is to safely deliver your passengers from point A to point B. You throttle up, speed increasing as you push toward the required speed to lift off.

All of a sudden, there's a pothole. Then another, and another. You can feel each passing bump in your seat and the controls. Each thunderous pound increases your worry of whether or not the landing gear is being damaged. You know they can put up with a lot, but these obstacles may be taking their toll. You make the split-second decision to abort the takeoff, regroup, and find a smooth runway.

As you're reading this, think about speed bumps in the form of people. You know exactly who I'm talking about. They are the loser friend, the loser family member, the annoying coworker, and any other person in your ecosystem who does nothing but talk shit, is overly opinionated about everything, and rarely has anything of true value or substance to add to your conversation. These are the individuals who, no matter how positive you are being or what progress (large or small) you are making in any aspect of your life, are the dirty sink sponges filled with bacteria, sucking out every piece of positivity you have left.

I am about to get very real here and I sincerely hope you put on your grown-up pants and take to heart what I'm about to say. If anyone in your life meets the description above, drop them. I am not kidding. I truly do not care if it is a family member or someone you've considered to be a "friend" in your life. People like this do nothing but breed negativity and bring down every single person around them. They are losers, they will live a life of mediocrity and regret, and, funny enough, they will somehow think that they are superior to those who have achieved infinitely more than they have.

Cutting these people out of your life doesn't mean that you feel that you are better than those individuals. Simply put, you are on a different path; a path filled with greater success than you can ever imagine and even bigger challenges along the way that will require significant mental and emotional strength and fortitude. The people I am describing will add absolutely zero value to your journey.

Over the last decade, my circle has become notably smaller. This isn't because I dislike people, or I don't find any level of enjoyment chatting with some of the people that I used to. Instead, I got to a point in my life where I knew myself better and I clearly understood the life that I wanted to build for myself. When listing out where I was spending my time and energy, spending time with those individuals simply didn't bring value to either side of the relationship.

Be prepared to lose friends. There is a saying that "It's lonely at the top." Now I'm not saying that you must wait until you're at the top of your field to begin figuring out who you need to be spending your time with. However, I view this saying as when you choose the path that will lead to an extraordinary life, it is often a lonely one.

Most people simply can't comprehend why you are doing what you are doing. Why you are working full-time during the day and working at night. Why you run multiple businesses during any free time that you might have. Why you care more about making your money work for you than spending your money at a bar on a Saturday night.

Here's the thing: in the process of making your circle smaller, people are going to talk shit. People are going to talk shit because they see you moving on with your life, growing up, and focusing on what matters while they, mentally, are still a tenth grader in high school.

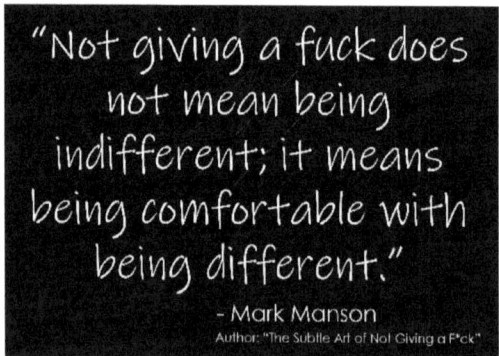

Those individuals usually know in that moment that, at the least, the frequency in which you're going to engage with them will significantly diminish, and because they are unsure of who they are and what they want out of life, their defense mechanism will be to project those feelings in your direction in the form of talking shit, telling people that you think you're better than everyone, and so on. Guess what? Until their opinion can be deposited into your bank account, it doesn't fucking matter.

A great example of this is my wife, Kim, and her decision to pursue a new career as a real estate agent. At the time, she was making $75,000 a year in a safe government job with great benefits and lifetime job security, for the most part. She had worked very hard to get to that point, earning a master's degree in her given field, and even left home for six months to train in another state.

Over the years, she got to a point that she realized the career path she was taking was her chosen path only because it was the safe path and one that society, family, and friends said would be the best option. It was at this time that she began to sell real estate in the evenings and on weekends. The number of times we both heard, "Well, you're not going to leave the government, right?" is immeasurable.

The spark Kim experienced in real estate was far brighter than anything she had experienced working for the government up to that point. So, what did she do? She began to clear her runway. After her real estate business skyrocketed, we sat down together and, as a team, made the decision for her to jump in with both feet. She had proven the amount of money she can make and that, at the end of the day, what she was doing in real estate simply made her infinitely happier.

In making this decision, Kim knew that many of her friends and coworkers that were in the same field as her would likely move on in one direction, and she would go in another. This didn't mean that she cared any less for those individuals, but she simply knew that, at that point in her life, she needed to focus her full attention on her new passion.

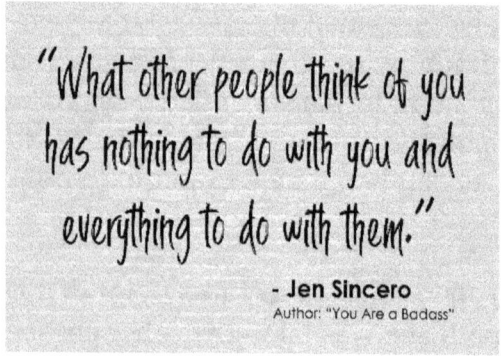

"What other people think of you has nothing to do with you and everything to do with them."
- Jen Sincero
Author: "You Are a Badass"

At the time, there were a lot of people who raised their eyebrows at the idea of Kim giving up this safe path that she had been on up to that point. The thing is, she wasn't giving up anything. She was taking ownership of her own destiny and doing what, in her heart, she knew was the best thing for her and her family.

On Kim's last day of work at her government job, a military two-star General inquired about where she was heading. When Kim told this individual that she was going into real estate, the General replied, "You know, some people just make crazy decisions."

Sounds like a pothole to me.

I can confidently say that Kim has never, even for a moment, regretted her decision. She has contributed to our lives at a level that is unfathomable by most people.

That $75,000 salary? It has now turned in to hundreds of thousands of dollars.

Kim set her priorities and cleared her runway. She became her firm's top new licensee her first year in real estate, and, during her second year, earned the firm's top ranking in her respective county. She soon became the top agent throughout the entire firm, all counties included and has done over $40 million in real estate sales to date.

Chapter 2: Nice to Meet You

I Am Not Special

Before we jump into the meat of this book, there is a foundational reality of who I am that I want to make crystal clear: I am not special. I will admit, I have had what I consider to be a fortunate upbringing. Not from a financial sense necessarily, but from the fact that I experienced the world from a young age due to my father's career in the army. I was surrounded by people who were successful in their lives and who encouraged me to do what makes me happy. Outside of that, I am not special.

I don't have an abnormally high IQ. I went to normal public schools. I did not go to a stereotypical Ivy League university. I don't have a trust fund that I've been able to use to fund my various interests. I am a deplorable test taker, and my eating habits consist of what you would find at a ten-year-old's birthday party. Side note, having money just allows me to buy fancier cheese.

This is so incredibly important to call out because you do not have to be what society or science deems as intellectually gifted to succeed. You just must decide what you want and then never stop focusing on that goal. That is what I did and continue to do, as my journey is far from over.

I decided the type of life I wanted and what I needed to do to get there. And since that moment, each and every day, I never waver on doing what I need to do.

Also, I give a shit. Plain and simple. Many people today don't care about what they are doing because they view it as a means to get on to the next day. Instead of planning for the next five years, they plan for the next weekend. As I said, I may not be the smartest person in the room, but I can promise you that no matter what I am doing, I sincerely care about the success of that venture and the success of everyone involved. That is called passion, my friends.

Passion. I have a passion for a lot of things. Primarily for building wealth, designing a life I love, and using my experiences to help others achieve their desired level of success, as well. I will discuss passion throughout this book and encourage you to read *About the Author* in the back of this book to see living proof of how passion can truly allow you to build a life you love.

As someone passionate about music, I learned to play guitar at age twelve, and by the time I turned seventeen, I launched a music production company called Right Beat Productions. I produced and sold instrumentals or "beats" to rappers and vocalists all over the world.

In 2015, I launched an affordable luxury bracelet company called Elite Wear. By the end of 2018, the company had sold thousands of bracelets, had clients in fifty countries around the world, a retail reseller in Italy, and a following of over 25,000 on Instagram—a group I proudly refer to as "Elite Wear Family Members."

As an FAA-certified drone pilot, in 2017, I started "Get It Sold Drone Services"—a company that provides unique aerial videography and photography for real estate agents and business owners in Omaha, Nebraska, and surrounding cities. This is in addition to a more traditional photography company I launched in 2018 called Aspects & Angles Photography.

Today, my wife, real estate superstar Kim Bills, and I own and operate Crucero Properties, LLC. Together, we purchase condos and single-family homes, add modern updates, and then offer them as rental housing units. As of 2019, we own eight properties with plans of acquiring at least five more over the next ten years.

Silver Spoon

We all know the saying "born with a silver spoon," meaning born with money or given money and things without having to work for it. We are also a society that loves to make broad, often inaccurate, assumptions about others who have money or live a lifestyle that is better than our own. An example of this inaccurate assumption is, well, me.

I can't count the number of times someone has made a backhanded comment about my success, or what I have earned in life as being a result of my father being a General in the army. Yes, I'm serious.

I remember a few years ago driving up to an event in my Mercedes, and an acquaintance saying in response to seeing my car, "Ah yeah, well, your dad is a General." Another time in a different situation, someone said, "Well, just call your dad; he can buy that for you." Similar comments from people have sprinkled their way in here and there over the years.

I generally don't care much about what people think of me, and I can brush most thing off fairly easily, but this was always something that puzzled me. Did those who knew me directly or knew of me through acquaintances assume that I could not live the life I had without sharing a checking account with my parents?

I moved out of my house and began supporting myself the morning after I graduated high school (literally) in 2006 at the age of eighteen. My father made Brigadier General (one-star General) in 2011—five years after I had already built a life for myself alongside my then-fiancé, now wife. I was already well on my way in my career, and building a healthy net worth, long before my father became a General.

To be clear, I am beyond proud of my parents and what they have achieved in their life, and I harbor no resentment as a result of a handful of idiots making presumptive comments about me. I could literally write a book about just how proud I am of my parents.

My point is this: remember, there is no quicker way to make an ass out of yourself than to assume you know something about a person without actually knowing them. Just as my father or any individual of higher rank in the military didn't just walk into a recruiter's office and slap a star on their shoulder, I sure as hell didn't just graduate high school and become a director.

Privilege

Here is the reality: I am a heterosexual white male, born a citizen of the United States of America to a middle-class family. In other words, I won the proverbial lottery. The feeling of not having food on the table each night or clothes on my back each day has never been part of my reality. I have never been turned down for a job or for housing because of the color of my skin or who I love. I have never lost a promotion because of my gender. No one has ever walked on the other side of the street at night to avoid me because of how I look. I have never been watched in a high-end department store as I shopped or been asked by a store employee if I realize how expensive the items were. I have never felt unsafe around a police officer or felt that the laws of our society, and those charged with upholding them, were not in my corner. My parents have never had to tell me to act a certain way around certain types of people for my own safety.

My basic rights as a citizen and human have never been violated or questioned by anyone, at any time, for any reason.

I have had my own struggles, many of which I will discuss throughout this book. And to be clear, I have not been handed the success I have enjoyed. Far from it, you will soon find. However, in a time when so many choose to blatantly ignore the underlying advantages they have had in life—even in the face of indisputable facts—I chose to recognize my privilege throughout my journey, and I encourage others—especially my younger readers who are the future of society—to do the same.

Chapter 3: Life as an Army Brat

Throughout this book, I discuss pivotal turning points and lessons learned over the years. But how I was raised, I believe, had a tremendously positive impact on everything I would do following childhood. As mentioned earlier, I grew up in an army family. That made me what is affectionately referred to as an "army brat."

Riddle me this: imagine yourself as a twelve-year-old. You've lived your entire life in the United States (the years you can remember, that is) — the land of the free, the home of the brave! The usual comforts of home are the norm, and you are naturally complacent with everything around you. You have malls, movie theaters, and endless restaurants at your disposal. You are heading into your teens, which are easily the most impressionable years of your developing young life. Then, you find out that you are moving to Germany. At first, it isn't that big of a deal because you are used to moving every few years but then, there it is.

What is "it"? Well, "it" is the feeling of anxiety—your stomach in knots, the sadness of realizing that you are leaving the friends you just made, the fear of what will inevitably be the first day of school in a place where you know not one other soul. Ahhh! It is almost too much to handle. The questions swirling through your head are mostly unanswerable, and you just want to put your face in a pillow and scream — and you do...more than once. It helps for a second but then all the feelings of fear come rushing back. Your parents are positive. They show empathy and do their best to ease your mind and help you understand why you are being uprooted once again, for what feels like the one-hundredth time.

Finally, the day has come. You've said your tearful goodbyes. You've stood in an empty bedroom that is no longer yours. Your suitcase is bursting at the seams as you drag it down the halls and out to the overloaded family car. The car starts and the journey to the airport begins. You watch out the window as the streets and houses you have found so comfortingly familiar for the last few years quickly disappear into the distance. In your mind, you are convinced you will never see those places again. There's no turning back. This is real.

The plane you board is bigger than you have ever flown in previously. You ask yourself, "What the hell is Lufthansa?" You proceed to your seat, and along with your family, you settle in for what is your new home for the next eight to nine hours. It's the longest, loneliest flight of your young life.

This was my reality as an army brat in 1999.

I don't remember much from the flight, but my first memory on the ground in Germany were the signs in a language I had never seen before. What a strange feeling. My dad had already relocated to Germany a few weeks before us and would be meeting us at the airport. That's right. My mother transported three rowdy boys, a pile of luggage, and a chocolate lab from Washington, DC, to Frankfurt, Germany. She's a freaking saint.

When my dad met us at the airport, I remember seeing him, in uniform as usual, excited to welcome us. The first thing I wanted was a Diet Coke. Anyone who knows me, then or present day, will not be surprised by this. I have an incredibly unhealthy addiction to Diet Coke. Hey, I could be addicted to some other types of coke so it's not that bad. I digress. My dad pulled out a few **deutsche marks** from his pocket and bought me a soda from a nearby stand. "German currency, great, another thing to learn," I thought to myself. But I had a soda, so I was a tad bit happier.

Up next was the drive to our new home. Let's see if I can accurately set the stage. Imagine a large hill. On that hill, perched at the very top, sat two structures. One was a hotel, and the other, my house. Surrounding these two structures was farmland with goats on one side and a German neighborhood on the other.

I remember being a bit taken aback by the size of our house. It was bigger than any previous house and certainly looked unique. It had a large flat area of the driveway surrounded by a brick retaining wall, and tall mature trees in front and back. The color of the house was a light desert tan with a big brown-wood front door. Hanging to the right of the front door, proudly and as if to send a message, was my father's army squadron's insignia belonging to the First Squadron, First Cavalry Regiment, or "1-1 Cav."

This house was specifically reserved for the squadron commander and his or her family. Looking back, it was a tad bit strange to have the commander's house by itself, on a hill, next to some goats and hotel, rather than on an army installation. Although, this was pre-9/11, so the concerns of present day didn't exist at that point — at least not to the degree that we know today. That would soon change, but we'll get to that later.

The house had an interesting smell. It was a mix between fresh paint and temporary furniture. I never knew temporary furniture had a smell but, it did, like something that has been sitting in storage. Our household goods would not arrive for a few more weeks, so the temporary furniture would have to do for the time being.

The house had five bedrooms and three bathrooms. There were also two kitchens, which was pretty cool. My room certainly wasn't large by any means, but like I had done so many times before, I made it my space.

After checking out my new house, I wanted nothing more than to call back to the states and talk with my friends. They had moved on with enjoying their summer, but I couldn't help but feel stuck in this strange limbo of denial and acceptance.

It sounds archaic writing this, but at the time, we had to use calling cards to make international calls. It was the year 2000 — the cell phone era was in its infancy, and our family computer had not yet arrived. The hotel next door had a payphone and I used it when I could. But it was often out of order, so I ventured out.

Why not use my home phone? What pre-teen wants to talk to their friends on the home phone in front of their family? As I ventured out, I found a phone booth about fifteen minutes away, positioned next to a road across from an old German military building and parallel to a current German police station. That would have to do. I completed this phone booth pilgrimage daily for several weeks that summer. Naturally, these walks to the pay phone would become less frequent and would eventually stop altogether. Life was weird. Life is weird.

The Duffel Bag

During your early teen years, it's normal for certain events to take place that are burned into your memory for a lifetime. Whether the event that was committed to memory was good or bad, that time is incredibly impressionable.

One memory that sticks out for me isn't a happy one, but I remember it like it was yesterday and it literally changed how society operates. When the attacks on September 11, 2001, took place, I was thirteen years old. I was still living in Gelnhausen, Germany, and had just come home from school that day. Due to the time zone difference, my school day was ending, but the horrific events were still unfolding stateside. *The Today Show* was airing on the Armed Forces Network (AFN), and like millions around the world, I sat and watched as lives ended and our reality changed forever. What none of us knew at that point was just how much life would change.

My house was not on a military installation. The commander's quarters at the time was located on top of a hill, next to a small American hotel, surrounded by farmland and goats. Needless to say, it was a pretty vulnerable place to be located and not knowing how the world was going to change after that terrible day, we were all on the edge of our seats.

Within a few short days, a guard shack was erected at the bottom of my driveway. Yes, I am serious. Staffed twenty-four-seven, a group of soldiers stood guard. They also performed exterior searches of my house.

I can remember sitting in my living room one evening and seeing a soldier carrying his rifle walk past my window. He was walking through the bushes and at his side was a military working dog. This would normally startle me or any other normal person on any other day, but during this period of unknown, I was simply thankful that they were there.

School was out for a few days while security at the installations and the logistics for American kids being bused in from neighboring towns for school was determined—a process we previously did every day without a care in the world. My morning walk to the bus stop—previously uneventful—now included a stroll past the American soldiers in my driveway, heavily armed, ready to do what they do. I recall being intimidated as I walked by, occasionally uttering a soft "hello," or "good morning." On a few occasions, I even I had to show my military dependent ID card just to get back up my driveway after school.

On the first day back to school, and for the following few weeks, getting on our school bus—which was a German city bus the US Government used to transport us to a neighboring post for school—was an experience in itself. Sitting in the left-side front-row seat as I walked on the bus was a soldier in full combat gear, heavily armed and keeping a watchful eye as we boarded. Once boarded and in our seats, we had to show our military dependent ID cards as the soldier walked up and down the aisle of the bus.

The security precautions did not stop there. Driving in front of our bus was a US military police (MP) vehicle and following closely behind was a German Police vehicle. I remember vividly how quiet the bus was. The sound of laughter and kids being kids was notably absent, as I imagine everyone was unsure what to think or feel.

Arriving at the army installation where our school was located was yet another surreal experience. By this time, the attacks stateside had been confirmed as terrorism, and as such, there was no way of knowing if other attacks would take place. As our bus approached the entrance gate, we sat in line with several other vehicles while the exterior and bottom of the bus were inspected for potential explosives and other threats. I wasn't thinking about tests, homework, girlfriends, skateboarding, guitar, what my friends were up to the coming weekend, or any other trivial things that make up the bulk of a thirteen-year-old's existence. Instead, we were all forced to experience the changing environment around us, the new norms and uncertainty.

After school, as we made our way off-post, I remember looking out the bus window and seeing flowers, American flags, German flags, and signs that the German community had begun leaving against the exterior chain link fence near the entrance and exit points. You have to remember, I was thirteen, and at that age, you just don't realize the history of the places you live, especially in an international community.

It was in that moment, however, when I realized that the German community was hurting alongside their American friends and neighbors and we meant much more to them than just the Americans who shop in their stores and support each other militarily.

In the following weeks, as I began to hang out with friends at neighboring posts, and as we all tried to figure out some sense of normalcy, I remember seeing something I will never forget. Next to the front door of a friend's apartment was a packed green army-issued duffel bag. My friend's father knew that the horrific event that took place weeks prior would likely plunge the U.S. and its allies into war. The duffel bag was there in preparation for when the call came. As many who donned the nation's uniform had done throughout our history, he was ready to leave at a moment's notice to defend everything we hold sacred. I imagine similar preparations were underway in many military homes across the globe during that time.

I have always been proud of our Armed Forces. Even at that age, I carried a sense of pride to not just call myself an American, but to know I was part of a military family. In retrospect, this image of that duffel bag sitting next to the front door of a house as kids and a spouse sat just feet away represented more than I could have imagined. They knew that the day would likely come for that soldier to pick up that duffel bag, exit the place they called home, and possibly never return. Unfortunately, this would be the reality for thousands of service members and their families over the next seventeen years. I often step back and think about that fact. At the time of writing this book, our nation has been at war for seventeen years. The same campaigns that started when I was in junior high are still underway at my age of thirty-one. That's a heavy fact to ponder.

One of the reasons I chose to describe at length the upbringing I had as an army brat is to help educate those who may not be familiar with what it's like to grow up in a military family. I remember going back to Virginia in December of 2001 on emergency leave with my family to visit my grandmother whose health was failing. I used some of the time to visit with friends I had moved away from a year or so prior. I remember one friend asking me, "Dude, did you hear about what happened on 9/11?" Now knowing what I shared in the paragraphs above, you can imagine my confusion at his question. As if me moving to another country would somehow place me on an island, cut-off from the events of the world — which is, ironically, what I also thought would happen before I moved overseas. However, as an army brat, I understood that not everyone gets it, and I politely confirmed that I was indeed aware of what transpired.

Although 9/11 was of the darkest days in our nation's history, it forced me at a young age to become more in tune with current events, to make an effort to understand cultures outside of my own, to be incredibly thankful for my life, and to move forward in life with a healthy amount of perspective.

Life Lessons from Skateboarding

There was no way I could write a book about key moments and lessons learned in my life without talking about skateboarding. From age twelve to twenty-two, I was an avid street skateboarder. When I moved to Germany in the seventh grade, a few of my friends had just started skating, so naturally, I joined in. Little did I know, this board covered in grip tape and rolling on four wheels would be like an appendage for the next decade.

Skateboarding is a culture. If you are a skateboarder, you know what I mean when I refer to this incredible sport as a way of life. For those not in the know, let me tell you: it's like speaking a language everyone in the tribe understands. It doesn't matter what language you speak, what neighborhood you live in, or how long you've been skating. When you are with other skaters, you all understand each other.

From the moment I stepped foot on that seven- and three-quarter-inch wide board, I was obsessed. Seriously. I lived and breathed skateboarding—constantly craving the feeling of cruising the streets, learning tricks and hyping up my friends. If I wasn't out skating, I was watching skate videos. If I wasn't watching skate videos, I was out skating. This was a daily cycle that never missed a beat.

I can still remember getting my first real board or "deck" and skate shoes. The deck was a Jamie Thomas model by the brand "ZERO" and the shoes were by a brand called "DVS." The deck featured an iconic photo of Jamie Thomas doing what's called a "smith grind" down a massive handrail. The shoes were all white and had a few blue accents if I recall. This was in the early 2000s when skate shoes were super bulky. I honestly don't think I could skate in them if I tried in present day. But let me tell you, I literally skated with those shoes until my left foot came through the hole that gradually widened from hundreds, maybe thousands, of attempts at learning a kickflip. I swear I went through two tubes of shoe-goo, pumping new life into them every few days. Ah, shoe-goo. Good times.

As mentioned earlier, I lived in Germany when I first started skating, and I am so lucky I did. I literally skateboarded around Europe with my friends between the ages of thirteen and fifteen. Who the hell gets to do that? My friends and I would jump on a train and explore every city and town, looking for new places to skate. The beauty of street skating is that everything around you is a skatepark. Ledges, stairs, handrails, embankments, curbs—it was all fair game! We would skate one spot for a bit and then move on to the next. Getting kicked out of skate spots by store owners or security guards was and still is a normal part of street skating. We, of course, were always respectful and left right away. Ha! Yeah, ok...

I remember going to see some of our favorite professional skaters when they came to town on tour. Tony Hawk, Paul Rodriguez, Bam Margera, Bob Burnquist, PJ Ladd, Jason Ellis, Eric Koston, Mike Taylor, and many others. I'm proud to say that my friends and I met them all. It was incredible. I remember how they thought it was pretty cool to see little American skate kids coming to see them in the middle of Germany. Funny story, somehow my mom snuck past security and ended up standing next to Tony Hawk. She leaned over to him and thanked him for taking the time to come out and put on such a great show for the kids. In my best thirteen-year-old voice: "Uhhh... Oh my God. Ok, Mom. Please stop talking to Tony Hawk."

So how did skateboarding teach me valuable life skills? Many things I learned were lessons that I did not quite realize until later, although others were more immediate. Most notably, the sport taught me about perseverance. In skateboarding, you attempt new tricks over time as your skills develop, varying in degree of difficulty. In most cases, especially early on, you will not land it first try. Second try? Nope. one-hundredth try? Maybe not even then!

With every failed attempt, you learn something new. Whether it be foot placement, weight distribution, angle of attack, or speed, you make small adjustments until you finally land it. When you finally land the trick you've been working on, there are few other things that give you a bigger sense of accomplishment. The only people happier than you? Your fellow skateboarders.

Yes, skateboarding is an individual sport in terms of the definition of a traditional sports team, but a large part of my energy and encouragement came from seeing my friends progressing and adding new tricks to their arsenals. I could always count on my friends to be ready to go skate and we collectively helped each other improve our skills. I credit these years to developing the aspect of my personality that is always encouraging those around me to succeed. For an individual sport, it sure as hell had the most mutually-supportive vibe than any traditional sport I ever played growing up.

Today, this hasn't changed in the world of skateboarding. Turn on any televised skate event or go to your local skatepark. You will see the pure love and encouragement each skater shows for the other. It really is a beautiful thing.

While skateboarding around Europe, the sport also introduced me to other cultures, people who didn't look or sound like me, and people who came from different socioeconomic backgrounds. As I mentioned earlier, once you stepped on that board, all the shit that in present day divides so many truly didn't matter to any of us. We came together for the love of the sport, to see each other land new tricks, and to just have a good time.

We were hungry teenage boys, so stopping at different restaurants around town was a big part of our adventures. We tried food from a melting pot of cultures and it was freaking awesome. There was a little doner kebab restaurant down the street from my house. It was owned by a Turkish family, and quickly became one of our frequent snack spots. After a long day of skating, my friends and I would stop by, grab a doner kebab and pom frits (French fries), and head back to my house to—you guessed it—watch skate videos.

It also didn't hurt that girls tended to flock toward the skateboarders. If you learn the history of skateboarding, that wasn't always the case, but I'm lucky that I started when I did! Ironically, for me, girls were usually the reason I stepped off the skateboard. Funny how that works. Listen, when you have the choice to make out with a chick or skate, you gotta do what you gotta do! I mean, my skateboard would always let me skateboard, you know?

Chapter 4: What They Don't Teach You in High School

High School Does Not Define You

I graduated high school in 2006, which, in retrospect, really wasn't long ago. My being raised in an army family meant that, like so many army brats, we would move to ten different states and two different countries over the years. It also meant I would experience more than one high school. In my case: four high schools between the United States and Germany. Looking back, it was an incredible experience, and one I did not appreciate until much later in life.

For some, high school is a blur. But for me, it remains quite vivid. So, what was I like in high school? I've been asked this question by coworkers, friends, and parents of those friends over the years, and my answer is not what you would think. Trust me.

Looking at my life today, one might think, "Two degrees, director-level job in his twenties, super successful wife, six houses by the age of thirty… he must have been a straight-A student!"

School would have been much easier if that were the case. My high school career from an academic perspective can be described in one word: shit. Well, at least the first two years. I didn't care to be there. I was rarely mentally present. I had no interest in college. All I really cared about was dialing in my 360 flips, Kanye

West's "College Dropout" album, learning the next guitar riff and, well, the usual things teenage boys focus on. I'm not sure how I passed the nineth grade, and tenth grade wasn't much better.

Fun fact: I failed Spanish in tenth grade. That was obviously a very bad thing, and I don't encourage it. However, looking back, it is slightly comical because my mom speaks and writes Spanish fluently, as she was born and raised in Venezuela. I never asked for help, of course, because I was a stubborn dumbass. I still laugh at that. Sorry, Mom! I mean, "Lo siento, Mamá."

I don't know how I was able to get my mom to agree to this, but I got my eyebrow pierced in the eighth grade. A friend of mine had one, and I, too, wanted to shove a needle through my face and hang a decoration from the hole. My dad was deployed at the time, so I am guessing that's how I was able to convince my mom to let me get it done, and get it done I did.

I was pretty thrilled about the whole thing. I went with the curved bar instead of a ring. It looked cool to me and my friends, and my girlfriend at the time thought it was cool. But that damn thing got caught on everything. Every time I'd put on or take off my shirt, somehow it would get snagged. A year later, the summer before ninth grade, I moved to Hohenfels, Germany. I was getting my haircut at the barbershop on post. The woman cutting my hair didn't speak very much English. I believe she was Russian.

As she was cutting away, she was having a conversation with the barber to my left. I didn't understand what they were saying but that didn't matter as I was off in my mind planning where I was going to skateboard after the haircut. Little did I know, I would not feel like skating that afternoon.

Out of nowhere—like a lightning bolt from Thor's hammer blasting me in the side of the face—I felt a sudden rush of pain shoot down the right side of my face. To my horror, the barber had accidentally caught the teeth of her black plastic comb perfectly on my eyebrow piercing, nearly ripping it completely out. We both shrieked, each asking, "What the fuck just happened?" but for what I feel were probably different reasons.

As if the blood dripping down my face wasn't awful enough, she grabbed some rubbing alcohol and put in on the ripped open wound. That was awesome and added no value to the situation, but what it did add was a considerable increase in pain. At that point, we were both comfortable calling the haircut finished. When I got home, I decided the eyebrow piercing—which was literally hanging by a piece of ripped skin, had a good run and it was time to come out.

One thing I am so incredibly thankful for is that I was able to just be a teenager. With an army officer as a father, some might find it surprising that I wasn't sheltered. I was allowed to make mistakes (within reason) and I had enough freedom to experience social situations that contributed to my development as a teen. Did I drink? Yep. Did I smoke? Yep. Did I succumb to peer pressure? Yep. Did I peer pressure others? Probably. Did I experience the stereotypical girlfriend pregnancy scare? Sigh. Yep. More than once. I am going to be honest—I have no idea how I made it out of high school without a kid. That isn't a brag, by the way. I just truly have no idea how I made it out unscathed. I have enough stories to write a trilogy.

Cigarettes aren't funny by themselves, but combine them with me at thirteen, and it's a smoking laugh. Once again, in Germany, I put myself in a tough position. I had just started guitar lessons with the wife of a soldier in my dad's squadron. A few sessions in, I shared that I was smoking cigarettes with my friends, and to my delight, the guitar teacher gave me a pack of cigarettes. Learn the basics of guitar and a free pack of cigs? I couldn't have been more thrilled. That happiness would soon be diminished, turning into fear and regret.

It was a Friday night. A friend and I were at a movie on post. This was a regular routine for us and nothing seemed out of the norm. I had just received my first cell phone. It was a pre-paid phone, pretty clunky and nothing special. Text messaging really wasn't a thing at that point, and it was more for emergencies or calling for a ride.

My parents knew I was at the movies, so when I noticed my phone ringing and saw their number on the screen, I knew I needed to answer. I plugged one ear to block out the sound from the movie and answered. On the other end was my dad's angry voice. In a tone I knew quite well, unfortunately, he said, "Be outside the theater in fifteen minutes." The call ended. No other information was provided. I looked over at my friend and said, "Holy shit. What the hell did I do?"

Looking back, not giving me a reason why I was being picked up so abruptly was a pretty gangster move on my parent's part. It forced me to sweat for the next fifteen minutes, going through the laundry list of bad shit I had done, trying to figure out what they knew and what they didn't. Screeching up in front, my parents pulled in and my friend and I got in the car. They still didn't say anything and took my friend directly to his house to drop him off. Once dropped off, it was on.

I don't remember their exact words, but they laid into me that they found out about the cigarettes my guitar teacher gave me. Like any parent going through this for the first time, they immediately began interrogating me about what other substances I may have been indulging in. Drugs? Alcohol? It was all on the table for discussion.

When we arrived home, we sat at the dining room table to continue the evening's festival of fun. I was drilled for what felt like a lifetime about my stupid choices — if I was doing drugs, if I was drinking, if I was a serial killer (kidding, I made up the last part but wow, these damn cigarettes seemed to have been placed on that same level). I remember my dad threatening to have the military police at our door in ten minutes to do a drug test. That didn't happen — and truly, they wouldn't have found anything — but the point was made. This probably explains my aversion to cigarettes and dining room tables.

My shenanigans as a youngster don't stop there. Here's more to enjoy! Picture this: a group of friends in Germany ages thirteen to sixteen who think they are God's gift to the world, piling into a charter bus to spend Spring

Break in a city just outside of Barcelona, Spain. The trip was one of many activities organized on the army post to enrich kids' experiences in Europe, expose them to culture, and so on.

What's the worst that can happen, right? Ha! Hold my beer. The bus ride was nineteen hours, and sweet baby Jesus, there were some questionable things taking place on that bus. When we finally arrived at the hotel in Spain, we quickly discovered that we were pretty much the only guests on our floor. There were chaperons, but not in our rooms. So, naturally, mayhem ensued.

In town, there were stores and street vendors selling a wide range of trinkets that were mostly targeted toward tourists like us. The item of choice for our group? Pellet guns. That's right, pellet guns. They were inexpensive, and the options were plentiful. We all had money with us, provided by our parents for food and activities, but when you are fourteen and you are faced with a choice between pellet guns, food, and an "I Love Spain" t-shirt, you choose the pellet guns. You always choose the pellet guns.

Sufficiently armed to the teeth and feeling kind of gangster, we headed back to the hotel. We waited for the chaperons' room to go quiet, at which time the lookouts at either end of the hall gave each other the "all clear" signal. Remember, this was in 2001, so we didn't have cell phones to text each other. Nope, we had to rely on good old-fashioned reconnaissance missions.

Then it happened. As if the hotel room doors were on a timer, they all flew open and each rowdy teenager flooded the hall, pellet guns blazing. By the way, these weren't child-friendly pellet guns. These things fucking hurt if they hit exposed skin. One side of the hotel hall rushed toward the other, both groups converging in the center as if they were two opposing armies slamming shield-to-shield, spear-to-spear in the middle of a battlefield. It was incredible. The vision of the floors covered in what had to be thousands of pellets still cracks me up to this day. The chaperons naturally woke up due to the spartan-like battle taking place just outside of their room.

Each pellet gun-wielding kid quickly retreated to their respective rooms, most of which had two to three kids in each. Like characters in a movie who knew they were about to be raided by the cops, we stood on the toilet and sink to reach the ceiling tiles in the bathroom. For what reason you might ask? We had to hide the pellet guns, and the ceiling was the perfect spot. We did our best to play it off as if nothing had happened but it's hard to disguise the still-rolling pellets all over the floor.

The next morning, down in the restaurant, the chaperons threatened to end the trip early if we did not turn in the pellet guns. Reluctantly, we handed over the arsenal. Have you ever seen photos from a war zone when the soldiers secure a location and confiscate a stockpile of firearms and heavy artillery? That's what the table in the restaurant looked like.

I wish I could say that was at the top of my list of poor high school decisions. Unfortunately, the list continues. My friends and I did some pretty stupid stuff. Actually, stupid is an understatement. Think back to when the

Jackass series came out on MTV. It had just started to air on German MTV and it quickly became a favorite of mine and my friends'. Not that I would blame my actions on a TV show, but we were most definitely in a "Jackass" state of mind for a solid year or so.

One of the funniest memories I have is with my best friend from childhood, Tito. Out of all of my friends from Germany, he's the one I've stayed closest with over the years. He was even my best man at my wedding over a decade later. In Germany, he lived in an apartment-style building which was the norm for most families there. In the basement of the apartment building was a long, dark hallway that stretched the length of the building. The lights never seemed to work so it was often something straight out of a horror movie. At different points in the basement were storage rooms and a laundry room. Give kids an empty room and they'll figure out a way to entertain themselves, and entertain we did.

We found an old broom in the corner of one of the empty basement storage rooms and a spray can of some sort of cleaning solution. I mentioned it was dark in the basement, right? See where this is going? We sprayed the broom with the cleaning solution and did the only logical thing we could think of.

Like The Goonies making their way through underground tunnels and finding themselves in need of a light source, we lit that broom on fire. After lighting it on fire, we proceeded to run around with it because, well, what else were we to do? Looking back, we could have accidentally burned down an entire apartment building!

No wonder parents always want to know what their kids are doing.

We then proceeded to the forest behind this apartment building. It was often used for military training. We found a canister of some type of fuel. So, of course, we poured a little on the ground and lit it up. I don't think I've ever seen flames shoot so high so quickly in my life. We both shit our pants and quickly threw piles of dirt on the flames to put them out. Once extinguished, we ran.

Did my parents nearly murder me for these situations I put myself in? Oh, hell yes. My point is that through all of these experiences, I quickly learned what to do—and more importantly, what not to do. Good or bad, I wouldn't change those years. I lived and I learned, probably more than most. I often reflect on those formative years and how they shaped who I became.

My early- and mid-teens were spent in Germany where I had a remarkable amount of freedom to cruise around multiple cities on my skateboard with my friends, eat in German restaurants, and interact with the locals. I chuckle to myself now when I see a friend's kid who is in their early teens, and I think to myself, "Good God, I was really that young just out and about in a foreign country."

I don't recommend waiting until the eleventh grade, but that is when I started to get my shit together. By this time, my girlfriend in eleventh grade—now wife—and I had been dating for a little over a year. I knew at that point that I would spend the rest of my life with her, and I credit her as being the main reason I got my head on straight and started to focus on what's important. I'm not a parent, and some might say they do not want their kid to be so focused on a boyfriend or girlfriend at such a young age, and I respect that. However, this is what worked for me, and I'm thankful that it did. With my head on straight and realizing I did not want my high school career defined by pellet gunfights and the like, I began taking things seriously and began making sure money and work were a priority, which has paid off significantly in my adult career by giving me invaluable experience.

Experience Matters

After tenth grade, my father's one-year tour in Carlisle, Pennsylvania had come to an end (as had Kim's father's tour there.) As goes with the military life, my father was assigned to a position in Virginia, and Kim's father was assigned to a position in Nebraska.

When I moved to Virginia the summer before eleventh grade, I was ready to begin earning money once again. Without having had enough time in the state to apply for many jobs yet, I found other ways to earn some extra money which would later pay for my plane ticket to visit Kim in Nebraska. What did I do? I spent a week in Woodbridge, Virginia with my aunt who had so graciously offered to hire me to landscape her backyard.

For those who are not familiar with the east coast summer temperatures, well, it was miserably hot. That didn't matter to me, though. Whatever I needed to do to accomplish my goal, regardless of how difficult, I made it happen.

Living in Woodbridge during eleventh grade, I soon got hired to work at TJ Maxx. They started me at $6.25 per hour, and my main job was unloading trucks in the back, sorting product and stocking the shelves. I can still remember taking my paycheck to the bank, standing in line, and feeling so accomplished to see the balance increasing. They did not offer direct deposit to high school kids at the time, and in retrospect, I am glad they didn't. It felt good to walk into a bank, stand in line and leave with a larger bank account than I came in with.

I didn't have a car at the time so every day after school, I walked across the street from my high school to the city bus stop and took the bus to work. Good old public transportation was an experience within itself. Standing at an uncovered bus stop in the freezing cold wind, rain, and snow is a quick way to build appreciation for the privilege of owning a car. Looking back now as I drive my E Class Mercedes, I am grateful for that experience.

My shift ended around 10:00 p.m. I would then head home to do homework, and then I'd do it all over again the next day starting at 6:00 a.m.. Though it wasn't a lot of money and I was pretty tired all the time, the job provided me with enough resources to fund my trips to visit Kim, who at that point had moved to Nebraska due to her father's new military assignment. That was really my incentive to get my grades up, as my parents allowed me to visit my girlfriend in another state as long as I paid for it on my own and kept my grades in favorable territory.

It was during this time that I really started thinking about my future — more specifically my future with Kim. The TJ Maxx I worked at was in Potomac Mills Mall, and in that mall, like most malls, was a plethora of jewelry stores. You can see where this is going, right? That's right, I wanted to buy an engagement ring. I saved every penny and eventually bought the ring, the same ring she wears proudly to this day. It was during a trip to visit me in Virginia that I asked her to be my wife. We then ran off to a courthouse and got married... kidding. Our seven-year — yes, seven-year — engagement had just begun.

The summer before twelfth grade was spent in Nebraska with Kim. I worked at the Fifty-Fifth

Communications Squadron at Offutt Air Force Base as part of a summer hire program. I literally scanned thousands of papers and then shredded them. It was tedious, but I was just happy to be there and to be earning money. I shredded paper to make some paper. Ha! My goal that summer: save my money to buy a car when I get back to Virginia. And I did just that. It felt incredible to walk into the dealership and leave with a brand-new car.

My senior year of high school, I had early release from school, so I was able to work more hours, which was perfect. I started working at the commissary at Ft. Belvoir, Virginia, assigned to the warehouse unloading and separating pallets of goods.

I mean no disrespect at all to those who do this for a career, but wow, this was tedious and tough work. If you've never worked in this type of environment before, here is a look into a typical day:

My coworker would unload the pallets of goods from the truck and set them down in our sorting area. Each pallet was about six feet tall, if not higher, and was wrapped in plastic to keep items from falling. Our job was to then remove the plastic and begin sorting products based on type. Each set of products grouped together would then be placed on a new pallet to be moved to another section of the warehouse, and taken out to the main shopping area to be stocked on the shelves by another team. I, along with my coworkers, completed these steps over and over until the eighteen-wheeler truck filled with goods, sometimes more than one, was emptied.

This type of work—which is very manually- and physically-demanding in nature—is important to our economy. There are currently upwards of 400,000 jobs in the United States as of 2017 that fall into a similar work environment according to the Department of Labor [1]. This book, however, is about doing what you want to do in life and focusing on what makes you happy and what inspires you to get out of bed in the morning. This type of work, for me, was not that inspiration. What it did do was inspire me to focus on education and put myself in a position to work later in life with my mind, instead of my hands, because I recognized that is what I wanted. Let's not get it twisted—the folks in that industry are probably better off with me not there, as anyone who has ever worked with me doing manual labor can attest to. I suck at it.

My point in outlining these high school job experiences boils down to one fact: it's up to YOU to decide whether or not high school will define you, and it is up to you to decide what experiences you want to gain during those four short years. In the grand scheme of life, high school is a tiny, insignificant blip. If you are a high school student reading this book, those four years may seem like it is all that matters. Trust me, it doesn't, and from a non-academic perspective, the day after you step foot into your first professional job or college class, this fact will quickly become apparent.

Whether you are having a positive or negative experience, one promise I can make is that life does move on, and it moves on quickly. For those reading this book who may be having a challenging time, read my next words and commit them to memory: that asshole who bullies you or the clique who thinks they are better than everyone, guess what? High school is it for them. They've peaked. How sad is that? The majority of them will be on a steady decline for the rest of their lives while you, if you so choose, will experience success on a level they can only dream of.

Focus on what is important to you. Focus on learning. Focus on being of value to others. Focus on how great you will make your future. Focus on experiences and learning, similarly to the lessons I learned from skateboarding. You can still have fun in high school and create friendships and memories that will last you a lifetime. The key is staying true to you, your morals, and your values.

Throughout this book, I touch many times on the topic of being of value to those around you, helping where you can, and so on. <u>Start today</u>. If you are in high school and see your classmate getting bullied, struggling in a class, or having trouble making friends, connect with that person and see how you can help.

Not doing this enough when I was younger is one of my few regrets in life. You never know; that interaction may lead to one of the most valuable connections you ever make in your life, and it will certainly prepare you for the "grown-up" equivalent situations you will undoubtedly encounter when you enter the professional world.

What You Should Have Been Taught

Much to my confusion and frustration, some of life's most fundamental skills are not taught in high school. Unless kids are taught the following by their parents or take the initiative to learn on their own, young adults are sent off into the world with incredibly low levels of financial literacy and life skills. To my younger readers, please take this section to heart, as understanding this extremely basic information will greatly increase the probability of you having a healthy financial future. We will touch on these topics later in the book, so this section will help us all obtain a common — albeit very high-level — understanding of the concepts.

How do I interview for a job?

Interviewing for a job is more involved than just showing up and shaking a hand. This is not an exhaustive guide on interviewing but here are the basics.

1. **Resume:**
The interview begins before you've even been told you have an interview. The process really begins once you've submitted your application, specifically your resume. If your resume looks awful, it will go in the trash. Again, if your resume looks awful, in the trash it shall go.

I have reviewed thousands of resumes over the last decade, and like most hiring managers, I know within ten to fifteen seconds whether or not I am going to bring the person in for an interview. I have seen some pretty crazy resumes. Colored paper? Yep. Multi-color text? Yep.

Misspelled words? Tons! Picture of a handwritten resume? Yep. Social Security Number and Date of Birth listed? Yep. Email addresses like BigSexyBeerFan69@gmail.com? Yep.

Seriously, though. Google "professional resume template" and you will have endless options to leverage. Messing up your resume is one of the most preventable errors in the process. Also, bring two copies of your resume to the interview — one for you to reference and one for the hiring manager. Even if you already emailed it as part of the application process, still bring at least two copies.

2. **Social Media**:
Clean up your social media or change all of your accounts to private. I don't want to hear the "What I do in my free time doesn't matter" argument. It is not at all uncommon for employers to take a quick look at an applicant's social media footprint.

If you are in the process of job hunting, be more cautious than usual with who is sending you "friend requests" on Facebook. It is not uncommon for potential employers to "friend" applicants as a way to gain a better glimpse into who the applicant really is. Keep in mind that not all social media platforms have the same privacy capabilities, so be vigilant.

That picture of you passed out next to the toilet after a party, shot-gunning a beer, or smoking a fat blunt? Go ahead and take that down.

3. **Test Drive:**
If you have an interview scheduled, and the location of the interview is at a physical location rather than a phone or video interview, do a test drive the day before. The number of applicants I have brought in who were late for their interview because they couldn't find the building is actually quite comical. I have even canceled interviews because the applicant was still out driving around trying to find where to go and, well, I needed to get on with my day.

I have always invested time in doing a test drive the day before my interview. Even if it's just a quick drive by to say, "Ok, there's the building and there's the area I am supposed to park. Cool." Doing this will also drastically decrease your nerves because you won't have to be worried the next day on your way to the interview.

4. **Dress the Part:**
This is not the time to dress down. Even if the dress code at the employer is casual, you don't work there yet. So, for you, it's professional dress. Remember, the interview is to sell yourself, and the interviewer has a very limited amount of time to decide if you are a fit, so you want to maximize that time as much as possible. If you look like a slob, the assumption could be made that your work is also sloppy. Google "professional dress for interviews" or search #interviewoutfit on Instagram for ideas.

5. **Know the Company:**
Spend twenty to thirty minutes researching the company you are interviewing with. With the information

we all have easy access to, there truly is no excuse for not having a general idea what the company does. The hiring manager may ask you, "What do you know about the company and what we do?" They are asking this to see if you did any preparation. If your answer is, "Um, I'm not sure," you can probably consider the interview a bust.

6. **On Time is Late:**
Arrive ten to fifteen minutes prior to the scheduled interview time, but no earlier. First and foremost, this shows that you are punctual. From the hiring manager's perspective, this is a small glimpse into how you might manage your time and follow directions in the future. Also, you may be asked to fill out forms when you arrive so having a few extra minutes to do that is always good.

7. **Don't Overshare:**
I know that we have become a society of oversharing with the prevalence of social media, but this is not the time. Remember, this is your potential future employer. They are not your friend. You are not in your living room. When asked questions about your previous work, your education, your goals, and other experiences, stick to those topics. Don't trail off on a tangent that leads to information that is inappropriate or not relevant. The amount of unsolicited personal, irrelevant information I have been told by applicants is astonishing. There are very few jobs I can think of where the most personal details of your medical history need to be divulged. Less is more, my friends. Less is more.

8. **Write It Down:**
Do not show up to an interview without a pad of paper and something to write with. Showing up with nothing to take notes on sends a message that you don't plan to note important information, and you may not be someone who prepares for client meetings and other important conversations. This happens all the time, and most times, I don't hire those people. Show that you give a shit.

9. **Don't Ask about Money:**
Nine times out of ten, this question will fall flat. Some jobs, especially if they are entry-level or a government job, will have the pay posted in the job listing, so it's much less of an unknown detail. However, when the pay is not listed, the hiring manager will either share the payment details in the interview or they won't. If they don't, leave it alone. That usually means that the hiring manager is working within a range, and their offer is going to be based on your interview, experience, education, and several other value-adding factors. You can always negotiate when the time comes, assuming you receive an offer. If the hiring manager asks you during the interview for your pay expectations for the position, have a number in mind. Be reasonable, but don't undervalue yourself. You know what you can bring to the table.

How do you determine what number to have in mind? As part of researching the company, you can also look on various websites, such as GlassDoor.com to gain a general idea of what the company pays for positions with a similar title to which you are applying. It also wouldn't hurt to determine, through your research, who the company's competitors are so that you can do the same pay exercise to gain a well-rounded understanding of what the general pay range might be.

Answering the interviewer's question about pay with a response that mentions the extensive research you have performed could actually win you points.

10. **Ask Questions:**
At the end of the interview, you will almost always be asked if you have any questions. Prepare questions ahead of time. It is a major red flag from a hiring manager's perspective if you don't ask any questions. Not asking questions sends the message—right or wrong—that you're not actually engaged or passionate about the opportunity. Think of three to four really good, insightful questions about the position, the company, valued skills for the role, and so on.

11. **Don't Ruin the End of Your Interview:**
Do not ask the hiring manager on the spot how you just did in your interview. I have experienced this from an applicant and have heard of other hiring managers running into the same situation. Trust me, all it does is make the interview awkward, and it reflects negatively on your level of confidence. If the hiring manager notifies you at a later date that you were not selected for the position, it would be appropriate at that time to inquire about what type of interviewing skills and experience you can gain for possible future consideration.

What is debt?

Debt is the money owed to a third party as a result of borrowing money that you did not have readily available to spend at the time. Debt may be in the form of credit cards, mortgages, student loans, and any other form of borrowed money.

Is there such a thing as good debt?

Though debt in the broader sense is viewed negatively, there is such thing as good debt. This opinion may vary by person, but I classify two types of debt as good debt: a home mortgage and student loans. I view these two as value-adding investments in your future.

Home Mortgage: Most people have to take out a loan to buy a house, simply due to the price of buying a house. This loan is most commonly referred to as a mortgage. This type of loan allows you to purchase a home without having to come up with hundreds of thousands of dollars in cash to make the purchase. Generally speaking, the goal of buying a home is to one day sell the property for a profit. This means the value of the home should increase while you live there, and you can then sell it for more than the original purchase price.

Student Loans: I will spare you a lengthy soapbox dissertation on why I think college is outrageously, criminally expensive, and will instead stick to the facts. I view student loans as positive debt because it is an investment in your future earning potential. The reality of the professional work world today is that a bachelor's degree is becoming the minimum requirement for many jobs. Having a bachelor's or graduate (master's) degree increases your earning potential, i.e. how much money you can make over the course of your career. The more money you make, the more quickly you can pay off your student loans.

What is a 529 plan?

A 529 college savings plan is a savings account created specifically to fund an individual's college education, usually that of your child. Why the strange name? Well, the 529 refers to section 529 of the IRS tax code, which was created in 1996. Section 529 provides several tax and financial aid benefits, such as being able to withdraw earnings down the road without having to pay taxes on the earnings.

What is an interest rate related to debt?

An interest rate is a percentage charged to the borrower, i.e. the individual(s) who took out a loan, usually charged on a monthly or annual basis. Interest rates can be fixed — meaning they won't change for the life of the loan — or variable — where they can, and likely will change in the future.

What is a fixed interest rate?

The answer to this one is in the name. "Fixed," meaning stationary or not moving, is, generally speaking, the most ideal type of interest rate. This is more easily explained with an example. Rebecca is buying her first home. The price of the home is $125,000 and she has been approved for the mortgage at a fixed interest rate of five percent.

This means that Rebecca will be charged five percent interest based on the amount of her loan, paid each month, throughout the life of the loan. Since she locked in a fixed interest rate, that five percent will not increase during the life of the loan.

What is a 401K vs. Roth IRA?

A 401k is a retirement plan that would be offered by your employer, whereas a Roth IRA is a plan you can individually open with a wide variety of financial institutions. If you have a set amount of money each month that you want to contribute to a retirement plan and you are weighing the options between a 401k and a Roth IRA, one of the easiest ways to differentiate between the benefits is by using the following phrase: Tax Today or Tax Tomorrow.

With a Roth IRA, you pay into the fund using post-tax income (i.e. money you've already paid taxes on). A 401k is essentially the opposite. The money you contribute to the fund throughout the year can be deducted from your payroll in a tax-free fashion. When you begin withdrawing from the fund in retirement, you will need to pay taxes on that money.

They each have pros and cons depending on the individual. Talk to your accountant or financial advisor to determine the best option for you. Keep in mind, depending on your situation, contributing to both simultaneously might make the most sense for you and your financial goals. We will discuss later in this book other non-traditional forms of retirement planning—such as real estate investing—in which case you and your financial team may determine neither of these options fit your strategy. However, ninety-five percent of the time, these plans do have a significant place in a well-rounded retirement plan.

Note: Unless Uncle Bob is a certified accountant or financial advisor, do not take advice from Uncle Bob. Financial advice should come from a financial expert who literally does this for a living. The tax code is over 10,000 pages and will likely change again by the time this book is published.

What is a Traditional IRA?

In the event you do not have an employer-sponsored 401k option, you may find a Traditional IRA to be a beneficial substitute. The intent is for a Traditional IRA to offer a tax benefit, similar to a 401k. However, your contributions likely won't be deducted directly from your paycheck prior to tax withholdings. Instead, the money you contribute to the Traditional IRA fund throughout the year can likely be deducted from your taxes at the end of the year, up to $5,500 annually. When you begin withdrawing from the fund in retirement, you will need to pay taxes on that money (similar to a 401k). Again, speak with a financial advisor and accountant to determine if this is right for you.

What is dollar-cost averaging?

Dollar-cost averaging is essentially buying shares of a stock regularly, regardless of the share price. (This can be in the form of buying into non-retirement mutual funds,

IRA's, and 401k.) For example, let's say I invest $200 per month in a mutual fund. Regardless of the market's current performance, that $200 investment is made without deviation. Some months, $200 buys a lower number of shares because the price of those shares is higher. Other months, the shares may cost less, in turn, affording me the opportunity to buy more. As explained by Investopedia, "The real value of dollar-cost averaging is that investors don't need to worry about investing at the top of the market or trying to determine when to get in or out of the market. Over time, the investor will end up buying shares at a price closer and closer to average."

How do I create a budget?

Creating a budget doesn't need to be a complicated process. In fact, one of the reasons so many fail at creating and sticking to a budget is because they overcomplicate the process. It's a simple formula really. First, answer two critical questions:

1. How much money is coming in?

2. How much money is going out?

Personally, I prefer spreadsheets. Open a spreadsheet and list your sources of income or the money coming in, as well as the expenses or money going out. The key should always be to have more money coming in than you have going out, or else you will quickly find yourself in a hole. Let's use a few sample figures.

You take home a monthly income of $3,000 after taxes. Your monthly outgoing expenses, which you've listed out individually in your spreadsheet, add up to $2,100. That includes rent, cell phone, car payment, and so on. Based on those figures, you are left with $900 each month. You have taken care of all the necessities which must always be priority number one. That $900 can now be budgeted toward other things like paying additional money toward eliminating your debt, entertainment, contributing to your emergency fund, and so on.

What is life insurance?

Life insurance, which is one of the most important things to have in place as an adult, is a sum of money that is paid out to a beneficiary in the event of your death. The amount of money paid out is based on the amount elected by the policy owner. Based on that amount, the policy owner is generally required to pay a premium each month to whichever company holds the insurance policy.

Life insurance is important because it helps ease the financial burden that could befall your family as a result of them losing your income following your death. It's not the sexiest topic in the world, but ensuring your family is taken care of can remove a significant amount of worry from the shoulders of all parties involved, knowing that those you hold closest will be taken care of.

Most people think they don't need a life insurance policy until they're much older. Are you more likely to die of an illness at an older age? Of course. However, shit happens and people die. You can't assume that death is going to come knocking on your door after you've lived a full life; it's just not reality. Kim and I have had life insurance policies since we were nineteen. A major word of caution: understand the type of a life insurance policy before signing the dotted line. There are multiple types that serve very different purposes.

A great source for learning about the different types of life insurance is through the Insurance Information Institute (III) which you can visit at www.iii.org. They do a great job of clearly defining what can be a confusing topic for many. From my experience having life insurance, as well the information I've learned through the III, life insurance comes down to two basic groups: Term and Whole.

I remember what Term Life Insurance is by the word Term, or a set period of time. Let's say you sign up for a Term policy of twenty-five years. That essentially means that if you were to die within the twenty-five-year period of your policy, your beneficiary would receive whatever financial benefit was outlined in the policy.

I remember what Whole Life Insurance is by the word "Whole," as it covers you for your whole life. Even if you were to live to 115 (congrats, by the way, if that's the case), your Whole Life Insurance would pay out upon the event of your death.

Do I need to plan for retirement this early?

I get it. When you are in high school — or even your early twenties — retirement seems so far in the future that its level of importance is often greatly diminished. I also hear parents say, "You can worry about that stuff later" and "You are too young to think about that." Holy shit, parents: STOP SAYING THAT.

Over the years, it has become abundantly clear that this mindset exists because many haven't taken the time to truly understand the monetary difference of starting now vs. starting later. Note: before I go forward, remember, starting to save for retirement at any point is better than not saving at all, so if you haven't started yet and you are in your thirties and forties, it isn't the end of the world, but you need to get your shit together. Ok, back to high schoolers.

Does starting early really make a difference? Yes. Holy hell, yes, yes, yes. In fact, it can be the difference between doing what you want in retirement or having to stick to an extremely strict budget in retirement.

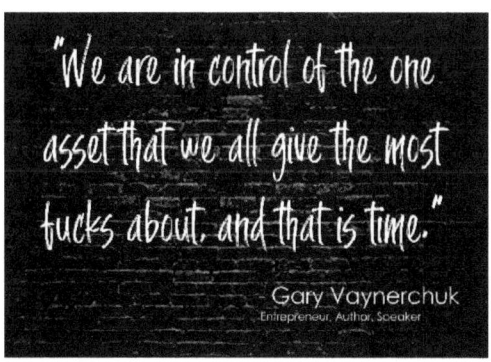

Ask yourself: do I want to pinch pennies in retirement, wishing I had more money, living with regret? Or do I want to not worry about anything other than enjoying life? It's a no-brainer, yet people continue to shit the bed in this area. Well, money talks, right? Let's look at some numbers.

First, understand the term "Compound Interest." The basic definition of compound interest is the growth of a certain amount of money over the course of time. Time is going to be a recurring critical factor here so pay attention. Below, Investopedia offers us a great example of how compound interest can work when your money is invested in a fund that yields a return on your investment [2]:

Let's say you start investing in the market at $100 a month, and you average a positive return of 1% a month (or 12% a year, compounded monthly) over 40 years. Your friend the same age doesn't begin investing until 30 years later, and invests $1,000 a month for 10 years, also averaging 1% a month (or 12% a year, compounded monthly). Who will have more money saved up in the end?

Your friend will have saved up around $230,000. Your retirement account will be a little over $1.17 million. Even though your friend was investing over 10 times as much as you toward the end, the power of compound interest makes your portfolio significantly bigger.

I don't know about you, but I imagine having an extra $940,000 laying around would sure come in handy during my golden years.

Your Parents Are Not Your Piggy Bank

Ok folks, brace yourself. The guy without kids is about to offer some opinions on parents supporting their grown children financially. Hang on to your seats. We have a noticeably concerning population of young people in our country who are overly dependent on their parents for financial assistance. Statistically speaking, if you are a young person reading this book, you may be part of that population and, frankly, part of the problem. But guess what? Your parents hold a good portion of the blame, as well. You won't be part of that problem after you read this book, right?

News Flash: your parents got you, or will get you, to the age of eighteen (or nineteen in some states). You are alive. You are healthy. You are able to work. It is time to cut the cord! Your parents — while they will probably always offer to help you whether they have the means to or not because it is the natural human instinct of a parent to help their offspring — should not be worrying about you financially at this point.

Take pride in getting your own place, paying your own bills, and standing on your own two feet. Your parents are at a point in life where they should be thinking about how they will spend their post-child raising years, not how they are going to continue supporting the rotten fruit on the branch that the tree can't seem to knock off.

According to a 2017 study performed by CreditCards.com, nearly three in four (seventy-four percent) of parents with adult children say they help their grown kids financially [3]. The study goes on to say that, of the support provided, eighty-four percent helped their adult children with living expenses, and seventy percent gave money to their children to pay down debt [3]. There are a plethora of similar studies performed by other entities that yield the same or similar results. What people rarely consider in these situations is how incredibly unhealthy of a relationship this level of dependency fosters, and the measurable impact it has on the parent(s) in their later years.

At risk of sounding like a hypocrite, I will say the following: being generous with your adult children, if and only if you have the means to do so, can be a wonderful gift, but there <u>must be limits.</u> Once those limits are established, there's no further discussion. The store is closed. The conversation is over. The failure to establish boundaries between parents and their adult children is what contributes to the level of unhealthy dependency that exists today. Once that line becomes blurred, parents, I promise you that you are not truly helping your child. In fact, you are contributing to their inability to own their circumstances, their inability to truly understand the value of a dollar, and their inability to be accountable for their decisions and consequences.

I am grateful to my parents for having instilled a level of accountability in me during my early teen years. My first job was bagging groceries at a commissary in Carlisle, Pennsylvania. I was fifteen, and a sophomore in high school. I only bagged on Saturdays and Sundays, and a spot on the bagging crew wasn't guaranteed on any day.

Picture this: every weekend morning, each kid who was hired as a bagger was lined up in front of the commissary before the doors opened. The supervisor would have everyone draw a marble from a bucket. After everyone had drawn their marble, the supervisor would draw one marble and whichever color the marble was, those with the same color could bag groceries that day. The rest of the kids would have to try again next time. This was a good life lesson that you can't get what you want just because you show up.

Fun story: well, not fun for me, but possibly fun for you to read. At this time, I had just moved back to the states from Germany. I made the rookie mistake of using my house phone to place calls back to friends in Germany. My parents were none too thrilled when a phone bill for well over $600 arrived in the mail. Did I get grounded? Nope. Did I get yelled at? For sure. But what else could my parents do to teach me a valuable lesson? You guessed it. I had to pay it all back. Every damned penny.

Imagine the mental anguish that had on a fifteen-year-old. There I am, pumped to get picked to bag groceries. I spend most of my Saturday and/or Sunday collecting tip after tip. The day comes to an end, and my pockets are much fatter than when I started the day. Money was the key to having freedom; freedom to go buy the latest and greatest skateboard gear or take my girlfriend out to dinner.

Happy as a clam, I come rushing through the door at home, ecstatic that I made $75 in tips, only to be confronted by my loving mother, hand out, ready to collect. Not $50, not $70, but all $75. She was like a member of the mob. "You screw up, you pay the consequences. I'll collect again next weekend." Looking back, damn, that was a valuable lesson and I'm thankful to have been held accountable for my actions.

No matter what, I always went back, and I'm glad I did. Not just because of the few extra dollars I had in my pocket after paying off my debt to my parents, but because one of the cashiers happened to be the girl I would marry eight years later.

Let's Talk About College

So, Matt, I don't want my parents to be my piggy bank, but what about college? My parents didn't want me to carry the burden of student debt and they put money aside to specifically give me the gift of a debt-free education. Am I wrong to accept?

No. Before I expand on that answer, let me be incredibly clear about the following point. If your parents saved using a 529 plan or other channels with the sole purpose of giving you the gift of a debt-free education, consider yourself one of the luckiest humans on the planet. If you are a younger person reading this book, please engrain that sentence into every fiber of your soul.

If you are an adult who has received a generous financial gift from a parent or relative, you are most definitely part of the minority, and it is incredibly important to realize that fact.

I am speaking from the perspective of someone who has interviewed and hired 1,000+ people over the last decade when I say: don't go broke—mentally or financially—going to college. That's an interesting statement, isn't it? Allow me to elaborate.

First and foremost, I'm a proponent of post-secondary education. It helped shape the path I am on today. What I am not a proponent of, is the belief that the school you go to is the end all, be all driving force behind your job prospects. If all you are is the name of a school on a piece of paper, you have much bigger problems to address. Now, if you aspire to go to the handful of large firms who are stocked full of graduates from Harvard, Yale, Stanford and so on, by all means, make attending those institutions your goal.

However, what no one tells you is that the person interviewing you is rarely interested in you based solely on where you went to college. In fact, I'd argue that it's one of the last things most hiring managers consider in today's working world. The person behind the desk cares about your experience and the related results. The college aspect is a factor, of course, because it shows that you have a well-rounded education and that you can follow through with completing something. However, that piece of paper in the frame doesn't make the person. It isn't the one providing an update on a complex issue in front of a room full of senior executives. At the end of the day, that falls on you, and I can promise you, no one in that room is thinking to themselves, "I wonder what school this person attended?"

College is becoming increasingly expensive. When I was an undergraduate, I was lucky enough to have parents who were in a position to pay for my school, preventing me from having student loans for my undergraduate degree. However, as someone who worked full-time during the day and went to school at night, I refused to allow my parents to shoulder the full burden of my college tuition. After all, we have learned up to this point that our parents are not our piggy banks, right? As such, I paid $500+ per month in addition to reimbursing my parents thousands by taking full advantage of tuition reimbursement provided by my employer at the time.

As a nineteen-year-old just starting my professional career, that $500+ per month was a lot of money, but as someone who takes great pride in being independent and in being able to contribute, I wrote the check with a smile. I also failed math my Freshman year of college, so I paid my parents back in its entirety for that class. I pass, they pay. I fail, I pay. Seems fair! Imagine, I do multiple forms of math each day in my professional life. Who knew! I digress...

A college degree opens doors. Many companies and positions require a minimum of an undergraduate degree to be eligible for consideration. Whether you agree with that or not, it is a fact of today's reality. Additionally, there is a plethora of data showing conclusively that an individual's earning potential increases with each level of education they possess. Take a look at the chart below [4].

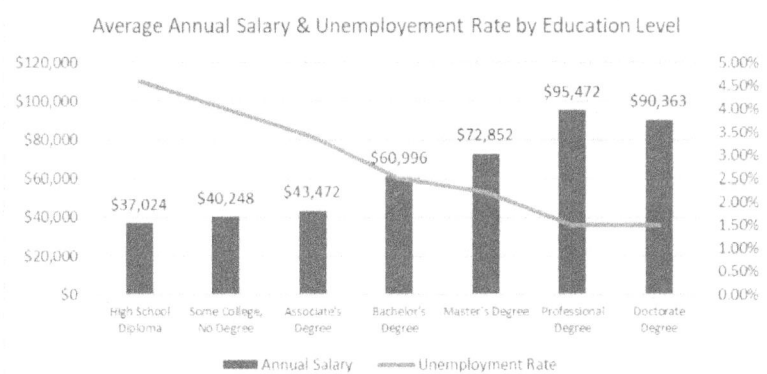

One of the best decisions I ever made was choosing to go to college at night. Personally, I did not care to experience living in a dorm or joining a fraternity or going to parties. I cared about one thing: starting my professional career, i.e. making money.

This decision turned out to be a key variable in my success. While my peers were going to school during the day, I was working full-time, gaining valuable experience, and building my work history. Work usually ended around 5:00 p.m. and class started shortly thereafter. Some classes I attended on campus and others were online. For the classes on campus, they ended around 9:00 p.m. I would get home around 10:00 p.m. and attempt to decompress before going to sleep. The next day, I would do it all over again. Aside from being tired, what other impact did the decision to be a night schooler have on me?

By the time I graduated in 2010, I had four years of solid work experience under my belt. That is four years in both individual contributor roles as well as supervisory. After all, my degree was in leadership, so I always looked for opportunities.

My wife also contributes her early career success to working full-time while going to college. During the first half of her college career, she went to school in person from 8:00 p.m. to 2:00 p.m. She then worked as an Emergency Dispatcher for ADT Security Services from 3:30 p.m. to Midnight. Were days long? Sure. Was it worth it? She will stand right beside me in saying every minute of it was worth it. Did Kim think that was going to be her forever-career? Nope. But she knew it was a stepping stone to where she wanted to go, even if that final destination wasn't yet clearly known. She soon achieved a promotion to a new position that would require her to work day hours, at which time she joined me in attending college at night while further pursuing her career full-time during the day.

Chapter 5: Be a Grown Ass Person

Put in the Time — Your Personal Brand Will Thank You

What is a personal brand? Your personal brand is essentially your reputation, your image, and how other people view you. I know that there is a fluffy notion that it is so incredibly important to not care what people think about you, but that is only relevant in certain aspects of life. It is not relevant when it comes to the image you portray to your employer and the reputation you make for yourself in your career. To be clear, it is important that you don't sacrifice who you are as a person, but you have to align your actions as much as possible with the acceptable culture that exists at your place of employment.

There are three different types of people in the workplace. Those who watch the clock, those who don't limit themselves by the clock and then those who fall somewhere in between. Whether I was unloading trucks in a warehouse in high school or leading multiple teams of over one-hundred people in corporate America, I often felt most comfortable not being constrained by business hours. The cliché of coming in early and staying late to get ahead, at least in my experience, actually worked in my favor.

I've always been keenly aware of what I do and say at work. Your personal brand can alter the trajectory of your career just as much as the results of your actual work.

Putting in extra time at the office and always being available to jump in after-hours helped influence my reputation as a dependable, dedicated, and driven young professional. Understandably, there has to be substance and reason for your extra work, but a notable amount of the confidence your boss will have in you is heavily rooted in your level of dependability and responsiveness.

Now, not everyone believes in this philosophy. Some believe in punching in and out at the same times, no more, no less and guess what? That's okay! Hell, some companies or the nature of your work won't allow you to work outside of business hours. Not everyone wants what you want out of life, and they're not any less important because of that fact. If their inability to be flexible creates an issue with their work, especially if you're their boss, that's an entirely different section of this book, and a good one, so keep reading!

Four Toxic Words: That's Not My Job

If you shudder and feel frustration in the core of your soul at just the name of this section, I share in that feeling. Imagine how I feel writing about it! There's a double-edged sword in the workplace that perpetuates delayed resolutions, frustrated employees, and angry customers.

If you have stepped foot in any type of workplace setting during your life, you will have heard the phrase: "That's not my job." It is so unsettlingly common for people to not want to do even one iota of work that is outside of their defined role. I refer to this as a double-edged sword because if an individual helps with the issue that's outside of their realm of responsibility, they could end up finding themselves in a tough spot because now there's a delay in their "regular duties" being completed.

Regardless of your position, you will be asked to do things that fall under the "other duties as assigned" part of your job description, and guess what? This will never go away. It's important to accept that fact early. Remember, while you are working toward success, you must be adding value along the way, and that value may be found in all shapes and forms. I have been on both sides of the desk for the last decade and reflecting on that time, there are four key practices that I employed that worked out in my favor in terms of career progression and my professional development:

1. Ask for More:
Want to get ahead? Be the person who asks or simply takes the initiative to do more. Don't get yourself in over your head, but if you have the capacity, put

yourself in a position to add more value while also gaining new experience.

2. You Represent Your Boss:

Carry yourself professionally in the workplace. Your words and actions are a reflection of your boss and trust me, your boss will receive feedback from others if you go off the handle. Whether you like your boss or not, take this point seriously. It doesn't make you a kiss-ass, it makes you a smart person who wants to grow and earn future opportunities.

3. Think Outside of Your Role:

No matter what career you find yourself in, you will most likely be faced with a multitude of situations that require you to think and act outside of the basic description of your job. There are very few professional jobs that can be successfully completed by working in a silo, either mentally or physically. Don't be afraid to take a step back and recognize that you are just one piece in a large puzzle that makes up your company. As such, you will very likely have to wear multiple hats. Know how to recognize boundaries, so that you don't find yourself overwhelmed. But don't be the person who immediately puts up a wall around their desk and refuses to play nice in the sandbox.

4. Lead from Where You Stand:

Having a title like "Supervisor" or "Manager" does not automatically make you a leader. Being a leader is not constrained by position or title. Anyone can lead. If you are in an individual contributor role, one way to lead is through your expertise. Just because you don't have a team reporting to you doesn't mean you can't stand up in a meeting and be the confident source of information that shapes policy and drives change. Assuming you do this constructively, and with a genuine interest in educating those around you, your colleagues will begin to see you less of an individual contributor and more of a leader.

The Four A.M. Warehouse

Warehouses seem to be a theme in my earlier work life, but this one was particularly unique and left a lasting impression. I was a staffing supervisor for a local staffing firm, and responsible for screening applicants and then placing them to work at a variety of different commercial clients. I drug-tested applicants, coached them on their interview techniques, hired them and fired them if needed. I was nineteen at the time.

One winter, a commercial client who specializes in meats and other foods needed two folks from our firm to be onsite in their warehouse during their busy season. My boss at the time presented the opportunity to me and I accepted. It sounded like a great opportunity to try something a little different and to actually be on a client site. The special assignment would last for approximately six weeks and little did I know, it would be the longest six weeks of my life. Don't get me wrong, I was grateful for the experience, but wow, it was rough.

Every morning, I would wake up between 3:00-3:30 a.m., as I needed to be at the warehouse by 4:00 a.m. Remember, this was winter… in Nebraska… at 4:00 a.m. Have you ever been punched in the face? That's how it felt walking outside at that time. I traded in my suit and tie for jeans and a winter coat for this position.

Armed with a clipboard with all the employee names, I would walk in and be posted at the entrance. As employees arrived, I would check them off the list. For anyone not present, I would call that information back to my office where one of my coworkers would then try to track them down. Once checked in, we got to work. Oh wait, I forgot to mention, the warehouse wasn't climate controlled. That's right. Inside felt like outside. Awesome. Really, really awesome.

So what type of work took place? Imagine a number of silver conveyor belts that stretch from floor to ceiling, all flowing to a central area. In that area, at the end of each belt, was a worker. Each worker would have a Styrofoam shipping box on a table next to them. Behind the worker would be a big tub of dry ice. Yes, a big tub of dry ice that slowly oozed "smoke" over the edge of the tub as if it were a witch's caldron containing a magic potion. It would have been way cooler if that were the case. Each worker, based on an order form, would grab the food product which was in a labeled box, put the dry ice in the Styrofoam shipping container, place the food item on top of the dry ice, close the shipping container, and send it on its way.

So, here's the deal. I was put on site to be a supervisor of the folks we hired to work there, but there was literally nothing for me to do once I checked in the workers each morning. Well, I'd feel pretty dumb just standing around with my thumb up my ass. There wasn't an office for me to sit in and work, and there weren't any administrative tasks to complete, so I did the next best thing: I untucked my damned shirt and got to work. Gloves, check. Safety glasses, check.

Don't worry, I'm not asking for an award because I rolled up my sleeves and dug in alongside the folks I hired. However, it was an experience… an exhausting one. Many of the folks I worked with did not speak English, which was fine, it just took a bit of navigating. I spent much of my time with a pallet jack, lifting pallets of product from one side of the warehouse and dragging them to another. I filled the shipping containers with dry ice, packed the boxes with product and helped load some shipments on the truck. Sounds fun, right? Eh...

Doing this day in and day out, I'll be honest, it was awful. Remember, I was nineteen so I was still attending college in person at night. I experienced a level of exhaustion that is hard to really describe. Each day was a haze. So what did this experience teach me? It came down to three things:

1. This type of work was definitely not for me. If anything, it inspired me to work harder back in the office gig so that I wouldn't end up in a freezing cold warehouse gig. No disrespect to folks who work those jobs, it's just not for me, and that's ok.

2. Many white-collar workers are the most spoiled pieces of shit in the world and have absolutely no clue how good they have it. You sit in a heated office with your phone plugged in to charge. Your headphones are on listening to your favorite podcast. You sip your Starbucks and have a little snacky snack for breakfast while chatting with your coworker on the other side of the cubicle wall. And you still have the audacity to complain? Get the hell out of here.

3. Work is what you make of it. There was a gentleman who worked for the commercial client — not for me — and his primary job was driving a forklift. He'd go into the giant sub-zero industrial refrigerator, grab a pallet of product, zip over to the drop-off point, and then zip back. He'd do this over and over again. While he worked, he laughed, he told stories, he sang songs, and it was quite funny to watch. Here we were in this freezing-ass warehouse at an ungodly early hour doing manual labor, yet this guy was making the best of it. He was happy to be working, collecting a paycheck, and being of value in his job. Most people who have it ten-times better in their work environments would complain that their chair squeaks.

Entitled to What?

While this applies to anyone at any stage in their career, I want to send a clear message to those just entering the workforce. Full disclosure, I'm going to sound like a lecturing old guy here. But if you're in high school, college or just entering the workforce, I'm talking to you, and despite the title of this book, start listening. I mean it when I say it: **get over yourself.**

You may not see it because you may not fall into this category, and if that's the case, the world thanks you. However, a large number of young professionals entering the workforce in the last ten years are incredibly entitled and expect to be CEO's on their second day in the office.

There are many perspectives I could write this chapter from. Whether I write it from the perspective of an adult, a people manager, a coworker, an entrepreneur, and so on, it really doesn't matter because the issue and its symptoms are all the same. Being entitled is probably one of the worst qualities a person can possess, and let me tell you, that quality is beyond noticeable. For my younger readers who may not be familiar with the terms entitled or entitlement, it is when a person feels that they should receive special treatment, have things handed to them without working for those things, or that they simply deserve certain privileges for, well, no substantive reason at all. It sounds pretty silly when you break it down to that level, doesn't it? Let's dig deeper.

Price of entry

You showed up to work. Congratulations. Do you want a prize? As a manager for the last thirteen years across three different business sectors, I have dealt with thousands of people both directly and indirectly. One of the trends that boggles my mind is the level of entitlement that exists in today's workforce. Who knows, maybe it's always been there, and I only noticed it when I entered the workforce. I'm sure that is the case to a degree but regardless, it's a problem.

You, my friends, DO NOT want to be part of that problem. I've observed people demand more money for marginal performance, and not understand why they didn't get it. I've observed new employees with little experience expect to be the damn CEO after two weeks. I've even observed people getting upset because they didn't get the job they applied for simply because "they applied."

Wait, you brought your mom?

Screech! Hit the brakes! Pause the music! I'm just going to say it: if a parent calls to schedule an interview for you, if a parent emails to inquire about a job on your behalf, if a parent calls on your behalf to inquire about the status of your interview or application, and, sweet Jesus, if you bring one of your parents to your job interview, we are done. You aren't getting the job. Period. I don't care how great your qualifications are.

I know many of you are thinking, "Wait, people actually do that?" YES! I have literally had someone in their twenties have their mom call me to follow up on their interview. This has happened more than once. I shit you not. Ready for some stats that will melt your face? Let's check out a survey completed by Michigan State University [5]. The purpose of the survey was to learn from employers how parents are getting involved in their adult children's pursuit of employment.

• Forty percent had dealt with parents who were trying to obtain information about the company on their children's behalf.

• Thirty-one percent had received resumes submitted by parents on behalf of their children.

• Twenty-six percent had contact with parents who tried to convince them to hire their sons or daughters.

• Fifteen percent had heard complaints from parents whose child did not get hired.

• Twelve percent had dealt with parents who tried to arrange their child's interview.

• Nine percent had contact with a parent who tried to negotiate their child's salary.

• Six percent had received calls from parents who were advocating for their child's raise or a promotion.

- Four percent had seen parents attend the interview with their child.

There are two audiences here: the adult kid and the parent.

Adult Kid: Punch yourself in the face. You are a grown person and you need your mommy and daddy to come with you to an interview or to call your potential future BOSS to ask how things went? I don't give a damn if your resume says Harvard on it, you are clearly nowhere near ready to work for me or any other person in the professional world.

If you are still allowing your parents to baby you to this degree, you will more than likely be the biggest pain in the ass to manage. You likely don't know who you are or what you want, your sense of entitlement is probably nauseating, you probably aren't accountable for your actions, and I wouldn't be surprised if you crumble under the slightest bit of pressure or constructive feedback. Are these assumptions on my part? Sure. But are they really? Maybe I should ask your mommy.

Parent: For the sake of everyone your adult child is going to encounter in life, STOP. Maybe you, too, are a pain in the ass to manage at your job, but I urge you to not pass on those habits to the future generation. Even if your adult child did a stellar job in their interview and then you decide to meddle and coddle and call the company to follow up, you more than likely just cost your kid the job. Well, the kid cost themselves the job by allowing you to follow up on their behalf, but you absolutely share the blame. You are not helping. Don't release entitled, scared little babies into the world. —Signed, The Human Race.

Trophies

Teens and pre-teens reading this book, the following is for you. If you were born in the late 1990s/early 2000s, you have been part of, to no fault of your own, a societal trend of being rewarded for participating in things. Not for winning them. Again, not winning, but simply participating or showing up. Your coaches, teachers, and even your parents may not tell you this, so Uncle Matt is here to give you the reality.

Up to this point in your life, you may have never been taught how to face adversity constructively, to grow from disappointment, or to truly fail successfully. You came in sixth in the wrestling competition? You received a ribbon. You came in eighth in your soccer tournament? You received a trophy for being there. You lost the debate in school? Here's an achievement certificate.

I need you to understand something before we go any further: participation trophies don't exist in real life. You aren't given prizes for just showing up. Don't get me wrong, being an adult is awesome and going to work and being of value is an incredible privilege so don't let my words discourage you. But your success over the course of your life will be infinitely more meaningful if you know how to understand and learn from failure.

To be clear before we move forward, we don't want to swing the pendulum too far to one side. I don't want to encourage parents to destroy their kid for losing, and I don't want kids to destroy themselves for losing. There is a balance, and my main point around this topic is that protecting people from failure helps absolutely no one. In fact, according to multiple studies, "When adults remove failure so children do not have to experience it, they become more vulnerable to future experiences of failure [6]."

I am a millennial. I'm not a bitter old guy who is going to write a chapter bashing millennials. But as I've done throughout this book, I'm going to tell you the truth based on my experiences in the workplace. And that experience tells me that there is a percentage of young people entering the workforce who expect a parade for clocking in on time. More concerning, many of those individuals don't know how to fail successfully. I know that term sounds counterintuitive but hang in there. I will break it down.

Let's press fast forward on your life about ten years. You are twenty-five years old working as a Sales Representative for a business consulting company. Your job is to meet with potential clients, specifically in the marketing space, and pitch to them why the consultants at your firm are the best in the industry.

The goal is to ultimately get them to sign on for several consultations over the next one to two years for a fee, and perhaps some sort of performance bonus if the client reaches a certain level of financial success following your engagement.

The day comes that you receive what is called a Request for Proposal, or "RFP," from one of the largest marketing companies in your city. You learn that your firm is up against four others in the proposal process, all trying to win this client's business. Over the last year, your firm has signed a few new clients which led to great revenue, but there were also some substantial losses. Your firm experienced client attrition due to competitive pricing, and you know that this new RFP could be a huge win—not just for your wallet, but the overall financial health of the company.

After a few weeks of compiling data, pitching ideas and answering their questions, you find out that the prospective client has decided to move forward with one of your competitors. You were top three but just couldn't pull ahead. As a result, you missed your quota for the year and won't receive your annual performance bonus. Additionally, the revenue from this deal was going to help your firm make up for some of the losses they had incurred over the last year. Now, without the injection of new revenue, Sally and Jim over in Accounts Payable are going to be laid off in an effort to reduce expenses.

This is a very real example of what takes place in corporate America every day. Coming in third place in the example above doesn't earn you a bonus, a trophy, or a ribbon. You did not win, and as a result, there are consequences—and, in some cases, life-impacting consequences like people losing their jobs.

Your boss trusted you with this RFP and underscored the importance of landing the deal. Now your boss is frustrated. If you have been conditioned your entire life to believe that coming in last should be celebrated, how will you learn to process this situation? How will you truly understand the gravity of the situation? How will you learn from your mistakes if you've never been told you made one? How will you move forward?

1. **Examine Your Case Study**

Ok, so you failed. You had a goal and you didn't reach it. You are upset. You are worried about your job. You are mad that you won't be receiving the commission at the end of the month. You just want to give up. Experiencing these feelings is completely normal. No matter how good you are at failing successfully, if you care about what you do, you will always feel bummed out if you don't meet a goal.

That term, "Failing Successfully." What does that even mean?

Failure is a part of life. No matter how smart or talented you may be, failure will creep its way into your life in some way, shape or form. How you choose to process that failure and use it to your advantage is what makes you successful. Winston Churchill once said, "Success is the ability to go from one failure to another with no loss of enthusiasm." Mr. Churchill couldn't have been more accurate. Yet, there you are, loathing in self-pity. Ok, allow yourself a minute (not an actual minute, but you know what I mean) to be bummed out. You are human. You have emotions. Go through it and get through it. Now, what you have in front of you is essentially a real-life case study to learn from. A case study from your own life! How about that?

Review what you did from start to finish. Using the consultant situation from earlier as an example, examine your client engagements including all of the information you provided. What data did you review? What was the feedback from the prospect on the data? Did you follow up and follow through on their questions and requests? Was that follow-up done in a timely manner? Was the information presented confidently and in a format that best highlighted the key points you wanted to make? Did you show any flexibility in your pricing? Was there even the option to show any flexibility in your pricing? Did the prospect share any key insights into what your competition was proposing? Did the prospect tell you why they didn't choose you? Did you ask?

2. Get Real with Identifying Opportunities

A major component of failing successfully is identifying improvement opportunities and accepting that opportunities for improvement do actually exist. Remember the kid who received the trophy for eighth place and was celebrated like a champion? What message did that send? Did that send a message that he or she needs to do better next time? That they need to train harder and focus more on a specific skill? That the team's ability to work together needs to evolve and improve? At least on the surface, I would say no. It sent the message that you can get eighth place and still be given the trophy.

Now, you're done asking yourself the case study questions asked above, right? At this point, you are ready to take improvement actions but before you do, it's important to identify internal improvements, and improvements needed in broader processes within your organization.

For example, if you were delayed in submitting answers to the client's questions, was that delay because you weren't managing your time appropriately? Or was the delay a result of other teams you were depending on for key pieces of information to be included in your answer? When identifying what needs to be improved, it's important that you are honest with yourself and those around you. If you messed up and it was within your control to prevent, own that fact and make the conscious decision to evolve, learn and prepare for the next time you are faced with a similar situation.

Let me repeat that, be honest with yourself. Many fail in multiple aspects of life because they refuse to be honest with themselves, most notably when it comes to areas they need to improve about themselves. I'll tell you this: the day you think that you can no longer improve yourself is the day "Game Over" pops up on your proverbial screen of life.

3. Create a Plan

One of my favorite sayings is, "Fail to Plan, Plan to Fail." It can be applied to a near endless list of situations in life, none more relevant than the topic at hand. At this point, you have asked the key questions and examined where the gaps in your process reside. You have had honest conversations with yourself and your colleagues regarding failures in current processes, policies and practices. The only way to see improvements come to fruition is by creating a plan. The plan should clearly state the area requiring improvement, resources to be involved in the process, an owner of the improvement item, risks to your business if not improved, and a projected goal date for completion.

One of the most common reasons improvement plans fail is due to lack of follow-up. That won't happen to you because you're going to stay on top of things, right? Right! Schedule a series of check-ins with the respective owners of the improvement items. Set the expectation early that these check-ins will occur regularly so that there are no surprises.

"Matt, how about the improvements I need to make within myself?" Great question. The same process applies. Nothing holds you more accountable to yourself than sharing where you need to improve with those involved in the greater improvement process. A friend, a family member, a coach, your boss, whoever. Tell someone what you are working on to improve and make it a regular part of your dialog. Be disciplined. Be dedicated. Hold yourself to a new, higher standard.

Quick story: I once received a low rating on one of my employee satisfaction surveys. It was mostly good but there were some areas I needed to improve. I was bummed out for a day, thought about it on the drive home, as I went to bed, when I woke up, and when I got back to work the next day.

However, I looked within myself, identified what I needed to change and then had a candid conversation with my team regarding areas I was going to work on. I stood in front of those who report to me and verbalized that hey, I am human and there are things I need to improve to more effectively do my job in area X.

Humbling yourself is where it's at, folks. It sends a powerful message not just to your own psyche, but to those around you. Now, the expectation was set. My team knew what I was working on and how I would get there. Powerful shit, my friends.

> "The difference between the real winners is how long they take to feel sorry for themselves. My winners feel it... but they come back up and say, 'hit me again.'"
>
> - Barbara Corcoran
> Entrepeneur, Investor, Business Consultant

Being humble does two things: it makes you appreciate what you have and the opportunity that exists around you, and it helps those around you establish trust and comfort with you. Conversations with someone who is down-to-earth are generally much easier to have than with someone who is arrogant and thinks that they are a gift to the universe.

4. Measure Your Results

Your improvement plans are finished, new processes are in place, you have formed new habits and actions that will help win deals, and you are ready to move forward. It's critical at this point to measure the results yielded from your improvement efforts. If you can't measure your effort, it's very difficult to identify whether or not it's working, what needs to change, and so on.

In the example at hand, measuring the number of deals won over the next six months following your changes in process would be one way to identify whether or not the changes are working. If the results aren't in line with what you were expecting, revisit the steps above.

Career Tip: this is also a great way to show your boss that you are capable of recognizing your improvement opportunities and can own that improvement from start to finish. Many are unable to do this. Your efforts will send a very good message.

Key Points:

1. Stop expecting to be given a parade for doing the basics. This is not real life.

2. How to fail is up to you, and that decision can have a profound impact on your life, career and those around you.

3. Parents, Coaches, and Teachers: find the balance between recognition and learning opportunities. Praising effort is great but ignoring where an individual failed helps no one.

Chapter 6: Dollars and Sense

Building Wealth

I am not sure exactly when this occurred, but terms like "money" and "wealth" seem to have been assigned a very negative stigma in our society. It is a popular talk track to link having money to being corrupt, an elitist, and out of touch with reality. Furthermore, the assumption is often made that those who have money inherited it, or by way of some magic or voodoo woke up one day with a fat bank account. What no one seems to ever acknowledge is the segment of the population who built their fortunes from the ground up.

While recognizing that stereotypes exist, I prefer to operate in the wacky wild world of facts and statistics. Through books like The Millionaire Next Door by Dr. Tom Stanley and countless other reliable sources, statistics show that approximately twenty percent of millionaires inherited their money, while upwards of eighty percent built their fortunes and are the first generation to enjoy those riches. That eighty percent became millionaires as a result of saving, investing, acquiring assets and creating businesses with multiple lines of income. Regardless, they are lumped in with the larger pool of millionaires—a fact they most likely don't care too much about because they are too busy, well, building their fortunes.

Before proceeding, I want to make something abundantly clear: money is NOT evil, and those who have it should be sources of encouragement and education for those wishing to one day be in their position. I do not live in a fantasy world where the bills are paid on hopes and dreams. To do what I want, live the way I want to live, and retire well before the national average, that takes money.

From my earliest memories, especially when I started making even the smallest amount of money, I have been obsessed. Is an obsession with money healthy? Hell yes, it can be. My obsession is built around the goal of having unlimited options in life, and that generally requires the almighty dollar. That is a concept many love to say they agree with, but very few take the steps to truly build wealth.

> "The law of concentration states that whatever you dwell upon, grows. The more you think about something, the more it becomes part of your reality."
> - Brian Tracy
> Motivational Speaker, Author

There are tens of thousands — probably hundreds of thousands — of books on the topic of finances, building wealth, investing and so on. I have read many on that list, and all of them have certain elements I have found valuable over the years. But what I want to share are the specific things my wife and I did and continue to do to build what we have today.

At our current pace, we will officially be millionaires by the age of thirty-five, meaning that we will have a net worth of $1 million or greater. In other words, if we were to liquidate all our assets, pay off all existing debt or liabilities, we would have at least $1 million in accessible cash left over. We are, of course, hustling hard to achieve that milestone even sooner. Knowing and tracking your net worth is incredibly important.

To be clear, I am not referring to the number of assets you have, though that is part of the equation. For example, if I were to define "millionaire" as the worth of your total assets, then we would have crossed that threshold some time ago. It is an exercise worth doing, as it is a great indicator of just how effectively you are building wealth and setting yourself for a relaxing, prosperous future.

The relationship you have with your significant other is the cornerstone of what keeps that union intact. When it comes to managing money, that is a job that must take place together in the interest of maintaining a level of mutual-support and continuing education. The world of money and business is vast and filled with challenging concepts and confusing direction, further underscoring the need to learn alongside your partner.

Philosophy of Saving and Risk Tolerance

There are two key concepts I want to focus on: Philosophy of Saving and Risk Tolerance. There is a wide range of beliefs regarding these topics, often differing from generation to generation. Your personal philosophy on saving and your risk tolerance are things you must identify within yourself and within your relationship with your significant other. This cannot be ignored. Let's start with some stats, as sobering as they may be.

According to a 2017 GOBankingRates survey, more than half of Americans (fifty-seven percent) have less than $1,000 in their savings accounts [7]. Based on the 8,000 surveys conducted, below are the results by dollar amount saved [7]:

$0 saved: 39%

Less than $1,000 saved: 18%

$1,000 to $4,999 saved: 12%

$5,000 to $9,999 saved: 6%

$10,000 or more saved: 25%

While that is an improvement from this same study conducted in 2016, there are still millions of Americans who aren't saving. If you fall into that category, here's where the tough love comes into play. Don't sit back and think, "Ok good, I'm not the only one." You need to sit back and think, "Holy shit, I need to get it together. I am literally one large unexpected expense away from financial implosion."

Like everything in this book, I am speaking from my personal perspective and experiences, and in my case, I have been with the same partner since high school. Naturally, my thoughts are driven by the power that comes from having a partner with the same philosophy on saving. So, what is our philosophy on saving?

Early on, a big part of our philosophy has always been about first understanding where our money is going. This may seem like an extremely basic concept, but it is one that many do not employ. I would venture to guess that if you were to ask a household, or even an individual, where their money goes each month, it would be difficult for them to break it down in an organized, factual manner. This is often how people get themselves into trouble. When you don't know how you're spending your money or where you're spending your money, you will end up spending *all* of your money.

Kim and I first moved in together in 2006 when I was eighteen and she was nineteen, and we saved as much as possible. Our household income at that time was approximately $51,000, or $4,250 each month before taxes, health insurance, and other deductions. In line with our philosophy of understanding where our money was disbursed each month, we sat down and put pen to paper. (Or, let's be honest, fingers to keyboard.)

- Rent: $725

- Two Cars: $325

- Car Insurance: $200

- Cable and Utilities: $284

- Cell Phone: $125

- Credit Cards: $0

- IRA Contributions: $250

- Reimbursing Parents for College Tuition: $500

To be clear, we didn't live on ramen noodles. We enjoyed life and treated ourselves when we could. What we never did was live beyond our means—a critical practice we employ to this day. If we didn't have the money to do something, we didn't do it. We never carried a balance on a credit card and put off buying a lot of different "wants" simply because we didn't want to impact our savings.

An example of this was my family going on a cruise that year. As you can imagine, my parents and extended family wanted Kim and I to come along, but the cruise would have cost us a few thousand dollars. Did we have the money in our Emergency Fund? Absolutely. Were we willing to spend a considerable percentage of what we had in that fund? No.

I'll be very honest, that sucked. I hated having to make a decision to not experience a fun event with my family because it would have had a negative impact on us financially. Rather than get down in the dumps about it, we used that as further motivation to stay focused on our career objectives and, in turn, our financial goals.

I come from a very generous family, and I was not surprised by the fact that one of my family members offered to pay our way, so that we could experience what we know would have been a wonderful trip. However, remember in chapter three when I talked about not using your parents as a piggy bank? Well, that same philosophy goes for *all* family members. I may have only been nineteen at the time, but I was an adult with an apartment and was standing on my own two feet. If we wanted to take a Caribbean vacation with my family, I wanted it to be on my own dime and not someone else's.

If you have a significant other, sit down with one another and understand each other's level of financial literacy, from basic 101 level concepts, to more advanced. The purpose of this conversation is not to make the other person feel dumb or blame each other for how money has been managed up to that point. The purpose is to evaluate, educate and manage moving forward. A newlywed couple or established with five kids, this needs to happen and needs to happen now. It will probably need to happen again next year, and the year after that, as life changes.

If the person in your home who is primarily in charge of the finances does not understand basic financial management or money growth principles, you need to seriously re-evaluate how money is to be managed within your household. Seriously, why are you allowing the prospect of having a healthy financial future drive blind at the wheel? Here are some questions to help you get started:

1. Do we both know how much money we CAN save vs ACTUALLY save each month?

2. Do we both understand where we want to be financially in two, four, six, or more years from this conversation?

3. Are we tracking our financial activity each month? If so, how? If not, why not?

4. Do we have an IRA, 401K, a savings account with our bank, and/or a 529 plan? Do we have any unnecessary debt? What is the interest rate on our credit card? And do we have a plan in place to pay off student loans?

5. Do we both understand what is listed in number four?

6. Are we doing anything to build our wealth outside of the traditional methods of saving?

7. Realistically, at our current pace, when can one or both members of the household expect to retire?

8. What are our risk tolerances, and how will we navigate our financial health if we are not each comfortable with the same levels of risk?

Have this discussion. Now. When it comes to money, walking the same path as your partner will greatly increase the probability of you, as a couple, becoming financially independent.

What does becoming financially independent mean? Simply put, it means building a financial infrastructure that allows you to do whatever you want and not have to depend on the income from a traditional job, too. For example, if you have monthly expenses of $2,000, and your side business, real estate rentals, or some other form of additional income amount to $3,000 per month, that "non-traditional" income can cover your normal expenses. Therefore, you no longer need to depend on working a traditional job. To be clear, that was a very basic example purely to illustrate the concept of being financially independent. In most situations, there are significantly more variables in play.

No one taught us anything. Seriously, outside of the basic, "it is smart to save money," no one taught us about investing, real estate, leverage, or anything else. Nobody ever sat me down and said, "Have you heard of this concept called Financial Independence?" We had to teach ourselves, and I am exceedingly happy that we did.

On weekends, when other eighteen- or nineteen-year-olds were out partying and getting drunk, we were sitting in our one-bedroom apartment in La Vista, Nebraska, scouring the internet, reading about different types of investments, how to grow your money, which types of funds perform the best, and how to determine such information, how to create passive income and what that means, and so on.

Remember that topic we discussed of entitlement and not expecting things to be handed to you? This is incredibly relevant here. We recognized that we had an endless supply of information at our fingertips, and we would have been crazy to sit around and hope that somehow that information would magically appear in our minds. It was during these first few years of our adulthoods that it became abundantly clear that the way of the baby boomers, also known as the creators of the bulk of the traditional advice discussed in our current society, is no longer relevant.

Think about that for a moment. Those referred to as "Baby Boomers" are part of the population of people who were born in the mid-1940s to the mid-1960s. A large amount—I would argue the majority—of financial management advice that we are indoctrinated to believe comes from the experiences of this specific generation of people.

Again, think about that. In 2019, during the most advanced time in our human history, countless people have entrusted their financial management and wealth-building beliefs to a philosophy that, more often than not, leads you down a path of working until you are seventy, instead of retiring when you are fifty, maybe even younger!

Baby Boomers: Make money, pay down debt, save money.

Me: Make money, leverage other people's money to make more money, and focus on multiple streams of income to become financially independent, all the while paying down debt along the way.

I don't know about you, but I sure as hell don't want to downgrade my lifestyle when I retire which is so often the case when people follow savings practices from the mid-1900s, if they ever even reach retirement, for that matter. Stop listening to the age-old retirement planning advice, and start planning for the century in which you're living.

Don't get me wrong, there is and will always be aspects of the more "traditional" savings practices that will always be relevant. That being said, financially speaking, in terms of setting yourself up for an extremely comfortable, worry-free retirement, leaning on the old ways simply won't get you there in today's world. My hope is that readers of this book span multiple generations. Regardless of your stage in life or prior financial blunders, making a change now can drastically benefit the rest of your life.

As you embark upon finding your savings philosophy and risk tolerance, I'm a firm believer that if you don't make mistakes, you're not trying hard enough. Mistakes are important. It is how we learn and grow. Unless we are talking about surgery. In that case, please don't make any mistakes! While I hate to admit this, you will make a mistake along the way with your money—probably more than once.

I am human as well, folks! I have very few regrets in life, but one that makes me laugh and cry took place back in 2008. I was about two years out of high school at the time of the recession. For those who are too young to remember, this was when the global economy faced its worst financial crisis since the Great Depression in the 1930s. The stock market crashed, home values plummeted, entire neighborhoods were lost to foreclosures, and there was a palatable amount of panic across our society. Financial institutions like Bank of America, Citi and others came crashing down. Citi, for example, had a stock price in excess of $500 per share prior to the recession. When things went south, their stock price dropped to an abysmal single-digit price per share. Are you thinking what I am thinking?

Remember when I mentioned my wife and I sitting in our one-bedroom apartment while teaching ourselves about investing? This was one of those times when our analysis told us that this was a once in a lifetime opportunity to buy a historically high-priced stock at a yard sale price. I mean, if the price recovered, it would be an astronomical return on investment. At the same time, nearly every conversation we would hear and every news outlet we would watch never talked about the potential upside. Instead, it was "the sky is falling" all day, every day.

We were twenty years old at the time and had a household income of around $50,000 and while we set aside a small amount each month to "play with," we were still figuring out our respective levels of risk tolerance. Nevertheless, we made the decision to purchase $2,000 in Citi's stock. I can still remember the pit in my stomach when we clicked "Buy." In the coming days, we watched the stock and, like almost every other company at the time, the volatility was enough to make you want to puke.

I previously mentioned the importance of understanding each other's risk tolerances. At this time in life, Kim and I had discussed our financial goals, but our understanding of each other's risk tolerances was in its infancy. To this point, we really had done very little investing in the stock market. As we continued to watch the stock market for the next few days, the shares we had purchased for $2,000 continued to drop in value.

Me? I was freaking out. That $2,000 was a tremendous amount of money for us at that point. Kim? She wanted to keep the money in and see what would happen. It was very clear that we weren't on the same page from a risk tolerance perspective and, ultimately, we decided with a degree of reluctance to sell the shares we had and recoup what we could. This means that our hard-earned $2,000 was now worth $1,100.

After selling our shares of Citi stock, we both experienced feelings of relief and frustration, but those feelings would soon transition into disbelief and regret coupled with a tremendous lesson-learned.

As has happened throughout history, the economy slowly began to recover, and companies whose stock prices fell to historic lows began to increase in value. Citi's stock eventually recovered to over $20 per share, then $30, then $40, and now to over $60 per share at the time of writing this book.

Doing the math, our $2,000 initial investment afforded us around 880 shares. The stock price, at the time of writing this book, is just over $64 per share. That means if we had held on to the stock, our original $2,000 investment would, today, be worth over $56,000. Instead, we sold those shares for a near $900 loss. One hell of a mistake, wasn't it? Most importantly, it was an even bigger learning opportunity and one that I am thankful happened.

As a side note—and this could be an entirely different book on its own—another financial collapse will happen. These things go in cycles and the human race is incredibly good at repeating its mistakes. I will never wish for the collapse of our economy because of the human toll that it takes, but Kim and I will damned sure be ready to take advantage when it inevitably happens again. A tremendous amount of wealth is created when the economy is at its lowest and those with high levels of financial literacy are the ones who reap the rewards.

Start Young

Hey teenagers and early twenty-somethings, I'm talking to you! I don't care if it's a paper route, bagging groceries, babysitting, coffee shop or you've just started a professional gig. Save and invest your money.

I get it. Money is the first sign of freedom to make your purchases without having to beg mom and dad. It's a cool feeling, and one you should be proud of. Now, set those feelings aside and focus.

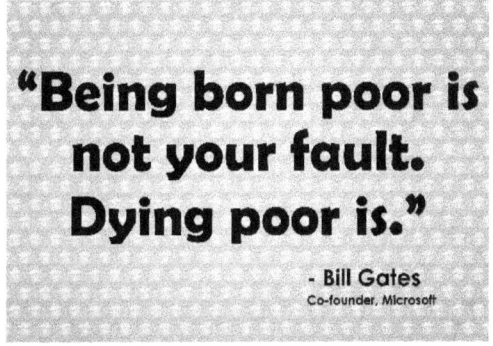

Have a goal. Your goal cannot be to simply make money. Sit down with your parents, a like-minded friend, a sibling, or even a teacher and define your goal.

Is your goal to save $2,000 by the end of sophomore year? Awesome! Perhaps your goal is to buy your first car by the age of seventeen using your own money. Even better! How much is the car and what will you do to save the amount needed? College coming up? Maybe the goal can be to contribute a significant amount to your tuition or additional living expenses. Sweet!

You get the point, right? Set attainable goals, put a plan in place, and achieve them. If you don't have a defined goal or set of goals, your likelihood of blowing through your money with nothing to show for it increases significantly.

Credit Cards & Building Credit

I am including the topic of credit cards in this book, not because they help you build wealth, but because they can easily *stop you* from building wealth. Let's get one thing out of the way: credit cards are NOT bad. I am not one of those people who avoid having a credit card at all cost (pun intended) or preach about how evil the credit card brands are. In fact, I believe that a credit card plays an important role in one's life IF it is used responsibly, e.g. as a tool, but not as a means to spend money you don't have.

What is a credit card?

A credit card is a small plastic card issued by a bank or retail store that allows you to purchase goods and services via a line of credit, e.g. without the exchanging of cash at the time of purchase. That purchase must be "paid back" or "paid off" when you receive your credit card bill or statement.

What is an interest rate?

An interest rate is a percentage applied to the amount you currently owe on your credit card. For example, a typical credit card interest rate could be approximately thirteen percent, though that can differ greatly based on the type of card.

Let's do some math: if I buy a t-shirt for $30 and do not pay it off in full at the end of the billing month, and my interest rate is thirteen percent, I will now owe $33.90. "Americans paid banks $104 billion in credit card interest and fees in 2018, up eleven percent from the prior year, and up thirty-five percent over the last five years. [8]" Talk about a sobering statistic.

What is a "minimum amount due?"

Listed on your credit card statement, this is a dangerous number. The minimum amount due is exactly what it sounds like. This is the minimum amount you must pay that month in order for your credit card to still be in good standing with the entity who issued you the card.

The problem with only paying the minimum amount due is that you will continue paying interest on the remaining balance. Many people can stay very comfortable only paying the minimum amount due until they end up paying insane amounts of interest. This is especially true if you have a high balance. The minimum amount due is going to stretch out for a very long period of time, and you will lose money by paying interest while the bank or store who issued the card will enjoy your extra money.

Should a young adult get a credit card?

Yes. In order to get approved down the road for a car, house — even a job in some cases — an individual needs to have a history of credit. Now, if you are eighteen and reading this book, your parents may not be encouraging you to get a credit card because they fear you will max it out, not pay your bill, and so on., and then you will come to them to bail you out. Side note: parents, I sincerely hope you would say a big fat "No Way" if they did ask. I digress...

So how can you control spending by using your credit card and begin building your credit history? When my wife and I were eighteen, we both got approved for a credit card. The limit wasn't anything substantial, but we didn't need a huge line of credit, so that was perfectly fine. Each month, we would buy something small like a shirt, pair of shoes, or a dinner date, and we would put it on our credit card.

The key here is that we did so with the full expectation that the card would be paid off in full at the end of the month. By paying it off in full each month, we incurred no interest and we started to build a pattern of full payoff, no late payment, no late fees, and so on. Fast forward today where our household income is drastically different than it was when we were eighteen—the practice of paying off our credit cards in full, regardless of the balance, has not changed.

Your credit history follows you… **forever! When it comes time to finance a car or a house, a credit report is pulled and your dirty laundry is put out on the table.** Use credit cards responsibly, and they can set you up for success.

Are you saying credit cards can *help* you build wealth?

A bit of a long answer, but here's one way we take advantage of credit cards to help us save and, in a way, earn money (the opposite of what a credit card company wants you to do). Use the Chase Reserve Card. Any money we spend is usually on our Chase Reserve Card, which we then pay off in full at month-end. This card provides exceptionally good "point" value on the types of purchases we tend to make. Those points add up over time and can be applied to future purchases.

To maximize our points, we make purchases through the Chase Portal, which is just an online interface into the normal online retailers that we routinely shop with (e.g. BestBuy, Dell, Petco, etc.). However, the key here is that by purchasing through the portal, we get "multiple times" points on every purchase.

Example: we buy our dog food from Petco. Rather than going into the store and making the purchase, we purchase it online and access Petco.com by going through the Chase Portal. As a result, this purchase grants us thirteen points per dollar spent. Do this frequently for purchases you're going to make regardless, and those points add up very quickly.

When we want to go on vacation, we book the flights and hotels through the Chase Portal. This allows us to apply our points toward the purchase. We have—not exaggerating—paid for entire vacations including first class flights with points alone.

See, there are two ways people view credit cards. One way is as a source to buy a bunch of shit you don't need, pay the monthly minimums, and eventually find yourself in a debt-filled hole with walls that continually collapse on top of you. The other way—the smart way—is to leverage the card's point system or other cash-back benefits to its fullest ability, enabling you to buy things without spending your own money.

There are many card brands out there and they offer very different benefits, so spend some time researching what will be of most value to you and your lifestyle. Kim and I spent an entire weekend mapping out the pros and cons between more than ten cards before deciding on the Chase Reserve Card. Make the decision that best fits your needs and goals.

Don't Have It? Don't Spend It!

Our society loves projecting an image of wealth and success. Most social media platforms are flooded with pictures of people showing the world how much they have. Now, I personally enjoy that aspect of social media because my brain views it as encouragement to keep working hard and eventually reach that level in life. What is troubling about our society in this regard is that a large portion of the population can't separate fantasy from reality, while also convincing themselves that they need to have what others have in order to be successful.

One of the most basic principles of building wealth is not spending money you don't have. (There are exceptions to this rule, of course, as we discuss throughout this book—specifically involving paying for your education or investing in real estate.) There's a famous quote, "Don't go broke trying to look rich." If this is you, please, stop it. I am not saying people should look homeless if they don't have an expendable income, but do you need the Louboutin Shoes, $250 Jeans, a Gucci shirt, and Chanel glasses?

When products are being thrown in our faces every second of the day, it can be difficult to turn away from temptation. If part of your ambition is to reach a level of financial freedom where you can have the nice house and nice cars, you will find that the road to that destination will be paved much more smoothly by not spending frivolously trying to make people think you have more than you do. I can promise you that all those people that you are trying to impress will not be by your side the day you go broke.

> "Most people fail to realize that in life, it's not how much money you make, it's how much money you keep."
>
> — Robert T. Kiyosaki
> Author: "Rich Dad, Poor Dad"

As I stated, I love the aspect of social media that shows the pinnacle of financial success, wealth, and access to some of the coolest things in the world. However, stop listening to the people in the comment sections or the voices in your head that are telling you that you need to spend your rent money on a new Swiss watch.

Chapter 7: Leading in Business

Own Your Destiny

One of the biggest differences between the rich and the poor is that rich people take ownership of their destiny, while the poor point fingers at others. The rich don't operate within a realm of perpetual excuses, self-loathing, and negative outlooks on the world around them. The rich take calculated risks and constantly pursue new opportunities.

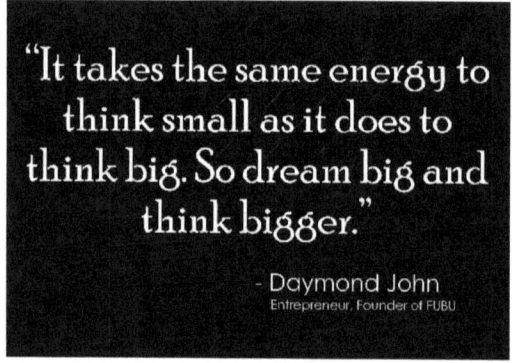

When there is a barrier in front of them, the rich think their way under, over, or through it. The rich recognize when something isn't working. And instead of throwing their hands in the air, they pivot, take what they learned, and move in a different direction. The rich don't let their weaknesses define them but instead, amplify their strengths. The rich don't wait for success to come to them. They reach out and grab it.

It's not uncommon to hear the following excuses, most frequently from those who complain about their current station in life — be it financially or otherwise. Part of owning your destiny is doing what you need to do to advance your life, as uncomfortable as it may feel at first. No one is responsible for the outcome of your life other than you.

"I can't find a good job in my area."

"Jobs around here don't pay enough."

"I didn't go to college, so I could never work there."

"Yeah right, I would never do that."

"Gross, that job is not for me."

When I was a senior in high school — eighteen years of age — Kim and I were planning for my big move from Virginia to Nebraska. If you recall from earlier in the book, Kim had already moved to Nebraska and started college, as she was a year ahead of me. During Spring Break, rather than going on a party trip or just sitting at home, my mother and I flew to Nebraska in search of mine and Kim's first apartment.

Side note: mom, you will never know just how much your support and encouragement meant to Kim and I. Seriously, I will buy you anything you ever want, ever, for the rest of forever!

Apartment hunting aside, I also used this trip as an opportunity to research job prospects in the area. After all, I would be straight out of high school and in a new apartment, so I obviously needed to have an income.

During the visit, and over subsequent weeks back in Virginia, I applied online and followed up via phone and email to multiple companies. I was able to secure a temporary government position as part of their Summer Hire Program. I believe the position paid around $10.75 per hour or $1,863 per month.

Let's stop here for a second. As an eighteen-year-old high school senior in 2006, I was able to secure an apartment in another state and find a job that paid the equivalent of $22,360 per year, which I would start within a week of graduating. This is where my sympathy tank for people starts to run on empty. As a damn teenager, I hustled enough to get an apartment and a job before I even walked across the stage to receive my diploma.

I am not looking for a round of applause, as in my mind, I was doing not only what I desired, but also what I felt was the appropriate thing to do. If a teenager with barely two years of work experience consisting of retail and unloading trucks can get an apartment and a job, why in the world do we have so many people — grown people — who fail to find opportunities and take control of their destiny?

The Bike Before the Benz

I understand how easy it is to want to reach a certain level in life quickly. The reality is that sometimes you need to ride a bike before you can drive the Benz. Accept that now and commit it memory.

Outside of my responsibilities of managing people, I am an incredibly impatient person. Right or wrong, that is who I am, and I own it. So, in some way, I understand not wanting to work an unappealing job. I really try to stay away from using too many clichés when offering advice, but on this topic, you have to do what you have to do. The key is doing it with a positive perspective.

Those first few jobs are an investment in your future. You are not above them, and they are not below you. Whatever the jobs may be, your employer is not doing you a favor by letting you work there and—reality check—you can likely be replaced in a heartbeat. You need to go in, day one, with the mindset that you are going to learn everything you can, you are going to be of value to your boss and those around you, and you must aim to develop all the necessary skills needed to succeed in your responsibilities. During this time, keep your eyes set on the future. Trust me, you will use the character and skills gained in the aforementioned positions to accelerate your success when you move into your long-term field of interest.

Dress the Part

The way you dress matters. It really, really matters, folks. Every company's dress code is different, but for the sake of this chapter, let's play it safe and assume that your office has a business casual dress code policy.

I discussed early in this book how important your personal brand is to your success. Your hard work — and the results of that hard work — are just part of your overall brand. Whether you realize it or not, your manager notices what you are wearing. No, they are not thinking about how those pants don't go with that shirt, or why your brown shoes are not complemented by a brown belt.

Realistically, they are thinking about whether or not they can put you in front of a client at a moment's notice if they can bring the higher-ups to your desk for an introduction, or if you should represent them and their department in a meeting, and so on. Yes, you guessed it. I'm going to use the cliché, "Dress for the job you want, not the job you have," even though dressing the part is so much more than a cliché.

Whether you agree with this thought or not, if you dress like you just rolled out of bed, someone who doesn't know you is going to think that your results are just as sloppy. If your clothes are pressed, fit correctly and show that you care about your appearance, someone who doesn't know you will likely have more confidence in your abilities.

Here's another cliché: "You only make a first impression once." Again, cliché but so incredibly true. Ask yourself: if the CEO dropped by my desk unexpectedly, will my appearance represent professionalism, care, and attention to detail? Or will my appearance represent someone who doesn't give a shit?

If anyone reading this is saying, "I don't have the money to..." STOP! I am not suggesting that you go out and buy a bespoke suit or Gucci heels. There are plenty of affordable options that you can find with very little effort. Go to your local TJ Maxx, Marshalls, or Ross and I can guarantee you will find a selection of clothing that fits the bill and will not break your bank. Even today, I literally wear some items of business clothing that cost me less than $10 from one of the aforementioned retailers.

Back to the "Dress for the job you want, not the job you have" cliché. When I was around nineteen, I once worked at a company with a casual dress code. It was a call center environment, and like most call centers, no one was expecting you to have lunch with the CEO, so what you wore was fairly lax.

Me? You already know: I wanted to be ready for that lunch. The members of management that I aspired to be like all dressed the part, so I dressed the part. It felt good to put on slacks, a nice shirt and a tie. It was my armor, my protection heading into the daily battle, and my brand.

What did my peers say? Some never said anything, which I never expected them to. Others gave me shit. "Why are you always dressed up?" "Do you ever wear jeans?" "I don't understand why you dress nice here." Nothing too heavy in terms of feedback, but still, they were questions that a less confident person may have listened to and changed their path in the interest of conformity.

Funny enough, the ones who were quick to share such unsolicited feedback, more often than not, had never gone past that same level in their career—the level I was working as a nineteen-year-old kid. Is there a correlation between their mindset and their lack of career progression? You be the judge.

Looking back on Kim's career, one moment that sticks out is when she worked at ADT Security Services at age nineteen and decided to apply for a promotion into another department. The requirement for that department was a minimum of twenty-four months tenure with the company. The position she was applying for was certainly a step up in both the pay scale and the hierarchy of the company, and although she didn't have two years tenure, she pursued it anyway.

In what was her current position, her performance was among the best, and the way she carried herself and dressed was often seen by those who were senior to her as someone who had ambitions of moving to a higher level. Applying for the promotion with only fifteen months tenure at the company felt like a long shot, but with her performance and the image she portrayed, it was worth taking the shot and, in the end, Kim was offered the promotion. Now, do I think she got the promotion because she dressed well? No. But would she have got it if she dressed like the shit? Probably not.

Emotional Intelligence

Today, having interviewed and hired over 1,000 employees over the years, I am often asked what I look for in a new employee, or what I feel are the most important characteristics to display in the workplace. My top answer has been, and will always be, Emotional Intelligence. In fact, one of the questions I ask candidates interviewing to join my team—at any level—is, "How important is emotional intelligence in the workplace?" The variety of answers I receive always fascinates me. How you answer that question largely depends on your understanding of what emotional intelligence really is.

Emotional intelligence, often referred to as "EQ," is the ability in which an individual can manage their emotions, identify emotions in others, and respond appropriately based on the situation. While not all situations are created equal, more often than not, people tend to react with emotion first and logic second. In some cases, the logic variable is completely absent, which we will discuss later in this chapter.

The key to EQ is switching those around, resulting in a reaction that is factual, reasonable and constructive. Now that you know the high-level definition of EQ, let's break it down a bit further.

According to Dr. Daniel Goleman, author of *Emotional Intelligence, Why It Can Matter More Than IQ*, there are five pillars of EQ:

Pillar	Definition
Self-awareness	The ability to recognize and understand personal moods and emotions, as well as their effect on others.
Self-regulation	The ability to control or redirect disruptive impulses and moods, and the propensity to suspend judgment and to think before acting.
Motivation	A passion to work for internal reasons that go beyond money and status.
Empathy	The ability to put yourself in his or her shoes.
Social Skills	Proficiency in managing relationships, building networks, and an ability to find common ground and build rapport.

Just by the general definitions of each pillar, can you see why EQ is so important in business? Admittedly,

EQ doesn't come naturally to everyone, and I won't pretend to understand the biological, psychological or hereditary factors that drive who we are or why we say or do certain things. However, what I do understand and have learned during my over ten years managing teams in corporate America, is that EQ can be developed over time. Regardless of your upbringing, life experiences, or predispositions, EQ can be learned and incorporated into your professional life.

Empathy is something people love to say they have and show, but rarely put it into practice. We want people to think we are kind, that we think about others, and that we take a person's situation into consideration when making decisions or passing judgment. But do we? Do you?

Using business as an example, it is rare that we can accomplish one-hundred percent of the responsibilities of our job without the support and assistance of others. When reaching out to a coworker for assistance, especially if they are on another team, it is important to understand the gravity of your request.

For those on the front end of their careers, please do not assume that your more seasoned or tenured coworkers and leaders will have high EQ simply because they have been working longer than you have. It is important for you to know that this will rarely be the case, further underscoring the importance of you developing EQ early. It is something that truly can be learned. This is scientifically referred to as "plasticity" when you practice new emotional intelligence strategies and, as a result, your brain and the way you respond to situations changes [9].

During my career, I have developed my EQ by taking close note of everyone around me, regardless of title. I paid close attention to what I should do and, more importantly, what I should avoid doing. It is incredible the things you can learn by simply paying attention to what is going on around you.

Key Tip: EQ doesn't know titles, salaries, the size of your house, or the price of your car. EQ can and should be applied whether you sweep the floors or run the company.

The first time I really recognized the two sides of the spectrum of EQ was during a meeting earlier in my career. I, personally, did not have much of a role in the meeting, and was there primarily to observe. As meetings sometimes have, there were a number of passionate opinions in the room, none more so than the two senior leaders at the table. What I noticed very quickly was that they both took polar opposite approaches to making their arguments.

On one end of the table was a leader who threw his hands in the air a lot, rolled his eyes as others were speaking, made it a point to ensure the volume of his voice was louder than everyone else's, and constantly swiveled back and forth in his chair in what most would consider to be an agitated state. He didn't like to let anyone else in the room finish their thoughts or make their points and, instead, spoke over them focused on doom and gloom scenarios, and continually attempted to bring the discussion back to what would be of benefit to him.

At the other end of the table was a leader who expressed his opinions and arguments in a calm, methodical fashion. He often looked to the subject matter experts in the room for their opinions, but what was most interesting was how he dealt with the leader at the other end of the table.

He, with what felt like surgical precision, attempted to understand the frustration and challenges that were most likely causing the other leader to act the way he was. He asked questions about the other leader's team and their workload, as well as how the topic at hand would either negatively or positively impact his team's ability to meet their objectives. Instead of focusing on all the negative outcomes, he asked the leader at the other end of the table how the outcomes would benefit the greater good.

In other words, he forced the other leader to step out of his very narrow-minded and negative bubble, and verbally acknowledge the benefits the situation would drive, despite the challenges faced along the way.

By the end of the meeting, the more constructive leader had certainly not cured the other leader of his lack of EQ. However, the constructive leader was able to use his own high EQ to disarm the other leader and further enable the decision-makers in the meeting to find a suitable path forward for the greater good of the company.

I have had the privilege of being a people manager for the majority of my professional career. One of the most entertaining aspects of managing people is that they are just that: people. These people are not robots. They have feelings and emotions. We all try our hardest to ignore what's going on outside of work in our personal lives, but inevitably, things bleed over. It is your job to recognize when this is happening and to use your EQ to manage it accordingly.

Success Doesn't Happen Alone

No matter how smart you are, no matter how skilled you may be, success does not and will never happen solely based on your efforts and your efforts alone. Even Tony Stark had help from Jarvis! Business is an ever-evolving machine and one that requires each nut and bolt to do their job. I have always had a keen sense of the importance of recognizing others for their contributions, but I have certainly stumbled along the way.

I recall working a highly visible project with a colleague who I respect greatly and still do to this day. I was so ingrained in fixing the issue that I failed to utilize words of inclusion like "we," "us," and "our" in my internal communications up the chain. As a result, the reader could easily have misinterpreted the direction and eventual solution to the problem as being solely my idea, an interpretation that would have been incorrect.

My colleague, who I was working with on the project, pulled me aside and addressed the issue head-on. Once I moved past the feeling of guilt and embarrassment, I was overcome with feelings of gratitude that he took the time to point out my flaw and cared enough to do so. That moment changed me, and I'm forever grateful.

One career-crippling move you want to avoid at all cost is becoming the person no one wants to work with. This applies to all industries at all levels. We all know the person I am talking about. Takes credit for other's work. Hates their job but won't leave. Views every situation with a negative reaction first. Always has a reason why something will not work. Low emotional intelligence.

Sound familiar? Now, to be clear, being someone who can work well with others does not mean that you need to compromise your integrity, contribute to a "group think" mentality, or not speak your mind candidly. The key is doing so with tact and purpose.

Rise to the Challenge

So, there I am, sitting in a room of approximately fifty other managers, associate directors, directors, vice presidents, and senior vice presidents. The room was akin to a large college classroom with stadium seating, a large whiteboard, and a podium. My boss is set to give a presentation on our operation to this rather large crowd of leaders, and then field questions on the content. She was scheduled to go on in about eight minutes. It was at this moment that she turned to me and said, "Hey, can you go ahead and present these slides?" Gulp.

After I picked my stomach up off the floor and administered to myself a form of mental CPR, I quickly scanned the slides and proceeded to the podium. Nothing terrible happened, and the presentation went rather smoothly. I knew the information, thankfully.

As I reflected on that day, it occurred to me that I was given this opportunity so that I may rise to the occasion and solidify myself and my personal brand as being nimble and ready to jump in at a moment's notice. My boss had enough confidence in me to represent her and our team, and I'm so incredibly thankful that she did.

Rising to the challenge is key to continued growth in your career, and it doesn't mean you have to present something in a moment's notice to a room full of leaders. It can be very basic things that are simply unknown to you at the time that the opportunity is presented or a task that everyone else finds to be too daunting.

One of the most disappointing qualities a person can possess — especially at work — is the immediate tendency to throw their hands in the air and not try. Sadly, you would be shocked — or maybe you wouldn't — at the number of people who give up and prefer someone else do whatever it is they were asked to do. As a leader of people, I promise you one thing: not trying sends a huge message to your coworkers and your manager, and it is a tough reputation to shake.

Some Days Suck

My career path from the age of eighteen has led me to a number of different management roles, starting as a team lead in the beginning, and currently as a director. I was always interested in being in a position that would enable me to positively impact others.

What many people fail to understand, especially those who have not served in a management role, is the tremendous amount of weight leaders carry on their shoulders. Now, I'm not saying this to garner any level of sympathy. After all, I made the choice to go into management, and I did so with my eyes wide open. However, especially for you younger readers, it's important to understand the perspective of those above you on the corporate ladder. In doing so, it will help you reconcile why certain decisions are made by your boss.

The heaviest part of the job? Firing an employee or laying people off. This part of the job is, hands down, the most difficult. I don't care who you are or how long you have been in management—if terminating someone's employment, be it for cause or otherwise, doesn't bother you, I highly recommend re-evaluating what you are doing with your life.

Even if the termination is for cause, you are still handing down a decision that is going to impact a human's life, and possibly the lives of their family. As such, it should be handled with the utmost certainty that the decision is the right one. For those who may be unfamiliar with terms like "cause," allow me to explain.

Most employers have policies covering a plethora of areas such as conduct, attendance, individual performance, and so on. You know that employee handbook your employer gave you? Please read it. If an individual violates a policy, or they are not performing per the expectations set forth for their respective position, and the individual has not improved after the concern has been addressed or the action was egregious enough, those situations may fall under the category of "cause." In other words, the reason for the termination was caused by the individual employee's actions.

Have I had to terminate someone's employment for cause? Many times, unfortunately. Most of those situations were a result of the employee's performance. In order to be successful, a company must achieve specific results. The individuals who drive those results are the employees. If the employee's work is not in line with the performance expectations set forth for their position, and that individual has been provided every additional tool, piece of guidance, and opportunity to improve, and they still don't drive the required results, it's time to make the business decision to part ways.

I have seen every reaction to a performance-based termination that you can imagine, even some that you can't. I have been screamed and cussed at. I have seen someone have a complete mental breakdown. I have had someone literally clear the contents on my desk onto the floor. I have had to call security to escort an individual out to the building. And the list goes on. Yes, this all occurred at a regular, run of the mill corporate America company.

Folks, imagine being a twenty-one-year-old firing people the age of your parents. That's some heavy shit to process. Nothing puckers your ass and snaps you into reality like being in that type of position. Age never meant anything to me in business, but I would be lying if I didn't mentally acknowledge how strange that situation is. I imagine the person on the other side of the desk was none too thrilled as well, but hey, it was what it was.

On a more constructive note regarding the way I recommend anyone in this tough situation handle themselves, some have simply taken accountability for themselves and their performance, accepted the decision, thanked me for the opportunity, and moved on. Truly, that is the minority, unfortunately.

Now, if you're in this position at any point in your career, I'm not saying just roll over and take it, especially if you know the decision to terminate your employment is illegal or unethical, in which case there are channels to address that. However, in most cases, the employer usually has their ducks in a row. Remember, wrongful termination is a big deal and carries quite a bit of risk for a company, both reputationally and financially, so you better believe the employer has dotted their i's and crossed their t's before taking the termination action. Sometimes people need to be grown up enough to know when they have screwed up and to accept the consequences.

Layoffs are a different situation and one I find to be the most difficult. Unfortunately, I've been the grim reaper for a lay-off and, well, it's about as shitty as it gets. For those just entering the workforce, a lay-off is when your employer terminates a position or a number of positions due to the company failing to meet or realigning their financial goals. This can lead to the company no longer being able to afford you, or deciding the position(s) is simply no longer needed for the company to move forward successfully.

In other words, the reason for the employee losing their job is outside of their control. Here's the deal, though it sucks: firing someone for cause is "easier" than a lay-off in my opinion. When it's for cause, you go into that situation knowing that the person on the other side of the desk is losing their job because of their actions. When it's a lay-off, in most cases, it's just a business decision that impacted them.

It's possible for cause to be hidden in a lay-off, as well. If the decision has been made to lay-off a certain number of employees, the decision-makers often look at the lowest performers in the to-be-impacted areas. So, technically, the individual is let go for cause, but it's often not communicated in that manner, instead saying it is part of a lay-off. The decision-making process can, of course, vary from employer to employer and industry to industry.

Sometimes You Have to Laugh

It's true, sometimes you just have to laugh. If you don't laugh, you'll cry! As you grow in your career, you will be faced with a multitude of puzzling situations. Some will be frustrating, while others will be downright hilarious. What will be common in each situation is that they will present learning opportunities that you will carry with you forever. Note, the examples below are not from my tenure with my current employer.

I once had to call a direct report into my office to address an odor issue, as I had received a complaint from other members of the team. Now, as a manager, I am trained to handle these situations with care, to not jump to conclusions, and to recognize that perhaps there's a medical issue in play. I explained to the individual why I called them into my office, and when I inquired about the cause, I asked if there had been any food left in the individual's trash can, or if they had perhaps heated up a meal in the microwave that might be omitting an unfavorable odor. The individual, with a straight face, replied, "Nope. I was just passing gas at my desk. I have a digestive system like anyone else."

This is a moment when having a speaking filter made of steel comes in handy. I reminded the individual that we must be respectful of each other's workspace, and to please excuse his or herself to the restroom in the future. I can recall walking to my car that evening, and stopping and saying to myself, "Yes. That was an actual conversation with a grown individual."

Are you a fan of oil paintings? I am! However, not so much in this situation. An individual in my department at the time once commissioned an artist to paint a portrait of himself. Just him. In an oil painting. He then hung the painting in his cubicle for all to see. It was a quality painting, but again, not something you usually see in an individual's cubicle. He eventually had to take it home because it became too much of a distraction for others in the department.

When I was eighteen, I worked in the staffing industry. As such, my position required the need to drug test applicants directly via mouth swab. In most situations, this was an uneventful process, but on occasion, I would encounter a gem or two. One day, I slapped on my latex gloves and proceeded to administer the mouth swab to an applicant I had just interviewed, as she appeared to be a good fit for a role I was working to fill.

A few minutes later, the results were in. Her test came back positive for marijuana. I headed back to the interview cube to break the news. Understandably, she was very upset, repeatedly swearing that she did not smoke marijuana. Part of my job was to educate and help applicants improve themselves and their career paths. After she calmed down, I asked if she was around anyone who smoked marijuana. She quickly replied, "Well, yes! My boyfriend smokes weed around me all the time!" I nicely replied that while I can't say for certain, that may have been how the marijuana got in her system. She stormed out of the office, and I can only imagine what happened to the boyfriend.

When I was eighteen, I worked in a local business' human resources department and was responsible for hiring both warehouse and call center positions. One applicant came in, and I took them through the process. This particular place of employment had the ability to run background checks that provided criminal history results within a matter of minutes.

When this person's results came back, their criminal history read like something out of a movie: multiple degrees of felony assault, kidnapping, false imprisonment, drug violations, and more. There I was, less than six months out of high school, and I had to take this guy into a cubicle by myself, knowing the types of things he apparently likes to do in his free time, and tell him that we were not going to be able to continue the hiring process because of the results of his background check. I'm not going to lie—I looked over my shoulder a few times walking to my car that night. I made it out of that one alive, so I guess I can laugh about it now.

Have you ever heard of someone hiding a goldfish in their desk? I have! I remember a rumor going around at work that an individual had brought in a goldfish and was hiding it in their desk. My employer at the time had a policy against such things, and as one of the managers in the department, it was my job to figure out what was going on and address it accordingly. Long story short, the goldfish was located and was asked to leave.

Last, but certainly not least, is a story about an individual, possibly more than one, who would spread their feces on the wall in the restroom at work, and once even on the carpet in the hall. Let me be clear, this was a professional workplace, not a prison, and I am not making this up. They were affectionately dubbed "The Mad Pooper" by a colleague, as no one knew who in the world could be committing these crappy crimes.

This mystery dumper would hit different floors at different points throughout the year with no specific pattern. Much like a serial killer, they would lay in wait just long enough for people to begin returning to their normal lives and then, boom, they would strike again. As of the publishing of this book, The Mad Pooper remains at large.

Chapter 8: Power of the Side Hustle

Do you have a side hustle? If not, get one. No, seriously. Not tomorrow, not next week, now! Why do I feel so strongly about this? First, allow me to explain what a side hustle really is. A side hustle is a business that generates income that is in addition to, or "on the side," of your main source of income.

For example, my main source of income comes from my director position, and my wife's main source of income comes from her position as a top real estate agent. My side hustles — Elite Wear, Get It Sold Drone Services, Aspects & Angles Photography, and others — while incredibly important, generate income that is used to fund other interests and allows me to do so while not touching any of our "principle" lines of income or savings. Let's break that down further.

Let's say there is a vacation my wife and I would like to take. The vacation is going to cost $3,000. We could use $3,000 from my wife's main source of income, but that would take away from the money put aside for savings and planned investments — specifically real estate investments in our case. We could take $3,000 from my main source of income, but that would take away from core bills, additional retirement savings, and emergency funds. How about an option to pay for the vacation using income that is not usually budgeted toward our living expenses, investments or retirement savings? Ding ding ding. You got it! The side hustle!

Now, your side hustle may not generate enough to take a luxury vacation (yet) but how about a date night or that new pair of shoes you have been looking at? You can also, of course, just save any and all extra income to further build your savings, emergency fund, and retirement. Gone are the times when an individual can depend solely on one income stream to build a healthy, sustainable financial future.

Most companies do not offer pension plans. If you are of the younger generation reading this book, you have probably never heard of a pension plan, simply because most entering the workforce will never have one.

A pension plan is a fund that pays long-time employees each month after they have retired from the company. These plans were commonplace in the mid-1900s. They skyrocketed between 1940 and 1960, but slowly tapered off in the late 1980s and early 1990s. During this time, people worked at a company with the mindset that if they stayed with the same company for more than thirty years, they would retire and collect a pension from that company as they lived out their golden years. Millions of older Americans still live off their pensions from "back in their day." Talk about loyalty, right?

Fast forward to 2019: you are on your own. The reality is, preparing for retirement is up to you, and the cost of living has no sign of decreasing. Building personal wealth in preparation for when you decide to step away from your core source of income is paramount to ensuring you can still live comfortably.

How do you get started?

There are a plethora of options at your disposal. Literally Google "How to earn additional income." You can take a more traditional route like getting a part-time job, or you can dive into the world of entrepreneurship which is comprised of a limitless expanse of directions one could go. Since my experience is more in the area of entrepreneurship, that will be my focus. Ask yourself a few questions:

1. Is there a product or service you are passionate about?

2. Can you offer a better alternative to that product or service?

3. Is there a product or service that doesn't exist today, but you wish it did?

4. In whatever you choose to make your focus, how will you set yourself apart in the respective market?

There are many other qualifying questions to ponder, but let's use a real-life example to get the ideas flowing. In January 2015, I had an idea to create a bracelet company. I noticed on Instagram that many people were modeling bracelets with their watches, and they were drawing quite a few likes and comments. I have a personal affinity for watches, but I didn't see any bracelets that I would want to wear. My wife had a jewelry business at the time, so I had her show me how to make a bracelet.

From there, I began sourcing materials that were more in line with my interests and desired look. I made a few initial bracelets and tested the waters on Instagram by posting a few photos modeling the bracelets alongside my collection of watches. Before I knew it, I was receiving comments and direct messages from people asking me where they could buy them.

Wait, what? People want to buy my bracelets? I mean, I hoped that would be the case, but someone is willing to give me money for something I created while sitting at my kitchen table? It was at this point that Elite Wear was born. Was it a fluke? Did I get lucky that someone wanted to buy my bracelet so soon after posting a picture of it on Instagram? I didn't know, and frankly, I didn't care. That first sale showed me that it was possible.

I created a free online shop (you can Google "free e-commerce store"), designed about twenty to thirty more bracelets, and launched the site. I was officially up and running. It was a very basic site, and I didn't even have a custom URL yet. The pictures of the products were amateur at best. Fun fact, for almost the entire first year I was in business, the product pictures were taken with my cell phone, on a white piece of computer paper, on top of the counter in my master bathroom. It was a sketchy setup, but it got the job done. You can actually see some of those original photos at the bottom of my Instagram feed if you have the patience to scroll for that long. I've posted over 11,500 photos at the time of writing this book, so good luck!

Keep in mind, at this point, I had maybe $300 invested in the business which included bracelet materials and shipping supplies. As interest in my product and resulting sales continued to increase, I invested every penny back into the business. I purchased a custom URL, trademarked the business name, created a custom logo, and expanded my materials. I improved my product photography by watching tutorials on YouTube, purchasing a light box (look it up), and using a real camera. Truly, I didn't take the few hundred dollars a month I was initially making and spend it on frivolous things. I invested one-hundred percent of it back into the business.

Fast forward to 2019: as I am writing this book, I've sold nearly 5,000 bracelets, I have well-known brand ambassadors across Instagram. A luxury watch store in Italy sells my products alongside some of the most incredible timepieces money can buy. I have clients in over fifty countries around the globe, and 25,000+ followers on Instagram (and growing!). I know my business is tiny compared to my competition but look what I was able to build in just over three years. It wasn't easy by any means, and it continues to be a daily grind. But it's a legitimate, growing and profitable business, all operating from my home office and by one employee: me!

How about this one? Get It Sold Drone Services. In 2017, I purchased a drone. I flew it purely recreationally but that quickly changed. With my wife being a real estate agent, the conversation of doing aerial listing videos and photos with my drone seemed like a natural direction. I came up with the name, created the logo with the help of an online logo generator, built a website using a pre-built website template, and got to work.

Within a few weeks, I was out filming properties for a variety of different real estate agents around Omaha and Council Bluffs. A few weeks after that, the FAA passed new regulations requiring me to obtain my Part

107 certificate in order to continue flying my drone commercially. I shut the business down for a few months while I studied for and passed the exam. After passing, I was back out flying the friendly skies!

From bracelets to drones, I share just two of my side hustles as examples of the wide range of possibilities you have in front of you. The emphasis here is to just start trying things. Write down some ideas, prioritize them based on what you feel is more realistic (i.e. likely to generate income), and then start figuring out logistics.

> **"If people haven't laughed at your dreams then you aren't dreaming big enough."**
> - Daymond John
> Entrepreneur, Founder of FUBU

Word of caution: remember to focus on you and what you're trying to accomplish and ignore the hate that will inevitably come your way, especially if you're trying something new. There are two types of people: those who bitch about what others are doing, and those who are the ones actually doing something. Be the one who is actually doing something. I got laughed at by both friends and family members when I told them I was making and selling bracelets. Want to guess how many of those same people now ask me for free product? Want to know how many of them receive free product? Take a guess!

Just Google It

We tend to fancy ourselves as this amazingly-advanced race of beings with endless resources at our disposal. Yet, at every turn, I see people who fail to use the resources in front of them to accomplish whatever it is they are working to achieve. Sure, I went to business school and graduate school where I learned a ton. I apply much of that knowledge in my day to day, be it corporate America or my side businesses. However, much of what I learned in business school was crafted toward being effective and adding value in an existing business ecosystem.

What if the challenge in front of you is to create that ecosystem? Well, shit. I would bet that many of you reading this book have long thought of an idea for a business. Those who know me personally, and have watched as I've launched company after company, may have thought, "How the hell is he doing that?" Keep reading and I'll melt your brain with how easy it truly is.

I started my first company when I was seventeen and a senior in high school. I had absolutely no earthly idea what the hell I was doing. I knew I wanted to create instrumental music or "beats" (i.e. music without vocals) and then sell that music to rappers and singers via multiple platforms including my own websites — MySpace at the time, SoundClick, and a few others. Remember, this was 2006 so Facebook, Instagram, YouTube, and others really weren't part of our lexicon at the time, at least not to the degree they are today.

The naming of the business was the easy part. I named it Right Beat Productions. "Don't buy just any beat, buy the Right Beat." Clever right? Yes, a bit corny and gimmicky, but still clever! I had the tools to create the music—as basic as they were at the time—but I was able to produce music that was of high enough quality that it could be sold to other artists, and I could be proud of the product.

Music? Check. Everything else? Google. I literally lived on Google for months learning how to create a brand name, how to trademark that name, how to make a logo, how to build a website, what free and paid channels were available to sell my music, how to best network with other artists and find platforms to get my music heard, and the list goes on and on. Message boards? Holy hell, I spent endless hours reading tips on message boards on everything from building websites to selling my music. I still do today! I even learned how to use Photoshop to create ads and design the layout for my website. I kept Right Beat Productions going for several years, working with many artists all over the world, and generating thousands in revenue in the process.

Did I get rich doing it? Absolutely not. However, I did have a hell of a lot of fun, I created a number of great friendships that still exist today. I learned a ton about business. And I was able to use the revenue to fund other interests. Side note: if you're following the timelines here, much of Right Beat Productions was built while working full-time during the day and going to college at night. What's your excuse?

Fast forward thirteen years...

It is 2019, yet the same fundamental challenges that I faced in 2006 still exist. I will be honest, it blows my fucking mind that people don't create brands and launch businesses because they can't figure out how. In 2019, there are no excuses. Zero. I am not a wizard at launching companies by any stretch of the imagination, but what I do have that sets me apart from other people, is the discipline to sit my ass down at a computer and fucking learn.

Consider this: today, there are hundreds, if not thousands, of companies that were created for the sole purpose of making the process of starting a company easier. I could absolutely scream as I am typing this to make sure everyone understands how incredible that is. In fact, my wife is probably wondering why I am screaming by myself in my office as I type this. Then again, maybe she's used to it. I am a pretty odd duck. I digress.

People, I can AND HAVE literally started a company from my phone. That's not an exaggeration to underscore how easy the process is. It is a straight up fact. "Ok, Matt. We get it. Stop screaming. It's easy. But for the sake of education, take us through it." Got it. Let's do it.

Invest in Yourself

Invest in yourself! This is a critical component I would be remiss if I did not shout it from the rooftops. There aren't many situations or statements that make me really need to channel my emotional intelligence, but of the short list of situations that exist, here are a few zingers:

"Nah, I don't want to spend the money on that logo."

"Nah, I don't want to spend the money on that material."

"Nah, I don't want to spend the money to hire an artist for that."

"Nah, I don't want to spend the money for that upgraded website template."

"Nah, I don't want to spend the money on marketing."

Sigh. I can't even count the number of times I have heard someone say they aren't willing to invest in their own business. What? Are you fucking kidding me? Let me stop here and throw out a non-negotiable.

IF YOU AREN'T WILLING TO INVEST IN YOUR OWN BUSINESS, BUSINESS IS NOT FOR YOU.

Smack yourself. Dunk your head in cold water. Do whatever you need to do to snap yourself out of it. If you aren't willing to invest in your own business, why the hell should anyone be interested in spending their hard-earned money on your products or services?

Now that you've changed your mindset and are ready to invest in yourself, here's how you can do it. Please know that this is not an all-encompassing list of every single step needed to build a successful company. My goal in providing the following is to show just how truly easy it is to lay your foundation. The hard work comes after.

1. Choose a Business Name

You know your product, service, or idea better than anyone. Therefore, truly the only person who will be able to come up with a name that fits best is you. However, a few softball suggestions are to make sure the name is relevant to what you're offering, the name is easily understood by your potential customer base, and the name is not already taken.

A great example of this is one of my companies, Get It Sold Drone Services. I had a drone, I had my FAA Commercial Drone Pilot Certification, and I saw a need in my local real estate market for aerial videos and photos. My main target client base were real estate agents. Well, what's the number-one thing a real estate agent wants to do? Get their listing sold. They don't want their listing on the market for an extended period of time — both for the benefit of their client and for their wallet. Naturally, Get It Sold Drone Services seemed like the perfect business name. When real estate agents see my advertisements, the name alone makes it pretty clear what service we offer.

When it comes to seeing if your desired business name is already taken, remember Google? Whatever the name is that you would like to use, type it into Google and see what comes up. You may have to do this multiple times with multiple variations of the name until you find a name that is not in use. There is also a multitude of websites specifically created to help you search for names that are not taken by existing companies — or even better, websites that will generate a company name for you. Again, just Google it. Found your name? Congrats!

Once you know the name, it's probably a good idea to trademark it. Depending on your business, how you plan to use the name dictates how important trademarking the name is. Personally, I don't like to leave it to chance, and I want to take every necessary step possible to protect my brand from potential competitors. As with anything legal, I recommend either consulting a local attorney or leveraging the countless online resources that are specifically created to help you legally protect your brand name. This process is not expensive and will likely cost, at most, a few hundred dollars.

2. Create a Logo

For me, this is the most enjoyable part of the process because it taps into my artistic and creative side. Your logo is going to be the symbol that represents your company. It can be an artistic representation of the name of the company, or it can simply be a symbol that represents the product or services. That is something you'll have to decide. No matter which direction you go, it needs to speak to you, and, more importantly, speak to your future customers. The greatest part about this is there is a plethora of websites that will generate a seemingly endless number of logo options for you to choose from. Did you hear that? You do not have to be an artist. You do not have to be an expert in graphic design. And you do not need to go and hire a marketing firm to create a logo for you.

Full disclosure, I am NOT paid to promote any of the following services, nor do I have any affiliation or financial interest in them, but here are a few companies dedicated to creating logos that I have successfully used in the past, continue to use today, and have nothing but good things to say about them. These websites include Logojoy.com, DesignMantic.com, and TailorBrands.com. These websites provide high-quality versions of your logo in multiple file formats that you can use for everything from T-shirts, to websites, to stationary, and any other swag that you feel will help promote your business.

3. Build a Website

This is one of the more time-consuming steps of the process, but your time is an investment that will reward you handsomely if done correctly.

Building a website, though daunting for many, is beyond easy in 2019. There are a number of incredible companies that can provide high-quality intuitive templates, enabling you to create and launch your website in a matter of hours. I've personally used companies like Wix, Weebly, Shopify, Wordpress, and others to create and host various websites over the years.

They all come with different features and cost structures, so you'll need to determine which aligns best with what you aim to accomplish. However, what they all offer are incredibly easy solutions to creating and launching a professional website.

Most of these companies offer *free* versions for a basic website, so no excuses!

Real Estate

Kim and I are real estate investors, and I suppose you can classify that as a side-hustle in addition to a retirement savings plan. For us, real estate investing has become a great source of monthly cash flow and will be an even better source of passive retirement income. While real estate investing is not for everyone, we found it is something we love.

We have no family members who have invested in real estate aside from their primary homes (at least, that we know of), and no mentor who guided us into this path. It wasn't a family business handed down to us. If there is anyone who can be credited to putting the idea of real estate investing in my head, it was simply the handful of times I heard my twelfth-grade marketing teacher in Virginia, Vera Woodson, refer to rental properties she had in Florida. Hmmm... That sounded interesting! The concept remained in the back of my mind over the next several years until Kim and I decided to give real estate investing a shot in the form of investing in rental properties.

What does that look like in a nutshell? Here is a real example. We bought a single-family, three-bedroom, two-bathroom, two-car garage house for $106,500. We purchased it with the plan to leverage a bank's money rather than our own. As such, we took out a loan via the conventional mortgage process. As an investment property, we were required to pay a twenty percent down payment which was fine, as we had been saving cash for this purpose. Our mortgage on the property came to $720 per month, which included principal, interest, property taxes, and property insurance. After updating the property, we rented it out for $1,350 per month. Based on those figures, we make $630 in passive income per month or $7,560 per year. That's $7,560 in extra cash, outside of our normal jobs and other businesses that we can save and eventually use for the next investment opportunity.

Now, imagine if you had five rental properties. For the sake of the example, let's say all five properties generate $7,560 each per year. That's $37,800 in passive income annually. $37,800 in cash! ten properties? $75,600 annually! *Hello!*

I honestly get butterflies in my stomach thinking and writing about this. The numbers above assume there are mortgages on the property. Let's say the properties are now paid off. That $720 mortgage on each property is gone, leaving only $300 in taxes and insurance as our only fixed monthly expenses on each property. All the while, that $1,350 rent is still in place, leaving us with $1,050 as passive monthly income moving forward. Drum roll, please.

Five properties? $1,050 x 5 = $5,250 per month, or $63,000 per year.

Ten properties? $1,050 x 10 = $10,500 per month, or $126,000 per year.

My friends, that's $126,000 that someone else is paying you to live. Do you have to account for repairs or vacancies? Of course! Just because your properties generate $126,000 in free cash flow annually doesn't mean you should go and buy a Ferrari. But how fucking incredible is it to have the opportunity to manage $126,000 in annual free cash flow? If you don't think that is incredible, you're either already rich or you're stupid. Let's call it what it is.

"But Matt, you spent $106,500 to make $7,560 per year. I don't get it."

"But Matt, you had to take out a loan to get that house. Now you have debt. Is it really worth it?"

I'm channeling my inner Stone Cold Steve Austin when I say, "Can I get a hell yeah?" A few key points:

1. I am not paying for the mortgage. My tenants are paying the mortgage. Someone else is paying off my debt. So did I really pay $106,500? A poor person might think the answer is "Yes." A rich person knows the answer is "No." Simplistically-speaking, I only paid that twenty percent down payment. The remainder of the mortgage is being paid by my tenants.

2. While someone else is paying off my debt, I am making several hundred dollars each month in free passive income. Think about this: I am doing very little — and some months, nothing at all — but I am collecting a check each month.

3. The house is now part of my portfolio of assets. I can keep the house for years to come and continue to collect passive income.

4. One day, if the market makes sense, I may have the opportunity to sell it and turn a profit based on the

original purchase of the house. This is known as "appreciation."

5. The passive income I make each month can be saved toward the down payment on another investment property. (That's right. Refer back up to number one. If I used my net rental income each month to save up the twenty percent down payment for the next property, sounds to me like I just bought a house without using <u>any</u> of my own my money!)

"Matt, you said you own six houses at the time of writing this book. Does that mean you have six mortgages?"

It does, indeed. Before your head explodes, consider the following. Our number-one rule for any venture we have is to not put ourselves in an uncomfortable position financially. In other words, even with six mortgages, in a catastrophic and highly unlikely situation in which all investment properties were vacant at one time, we would be able to pay for all of the mortgages using income from our non-rental property related income.

I want to discuss a few frequently asked questions as well as address some of the more common misconceptions about investing in real estate.

FAQ: How did you get approved for six mortgages?

I'll answer this first because, truly, the answer to this question is really the proof of concept for this entire book. A mortgage approval is predicated on your past and present financial health. My wife and I have built a decade-long track record of paying bills on time, not carrying a balance on our credit cards, paying down any debt we may have (car, for example), building and maintaining credit scores into the 800s, and having a healthy amount of cash-on-hand. I am not a mortgage broker by any means, but in a nutshell, a lender's decision of whether or not to lend you money is dictated by their confidence in you being able to pay back the money.

FAQ: If you have a healthy amount of cash available, why not buy the house in cash vs. taking out a mortgage?

A few reasons, with the first being that our strategy focused on leverage. We have the ability to leverage a bank's money as a tool to buy a property that will generate free cash flow to us while our tenants pay off the loan, all while not depleting our cash-on-hand, which is saved and used for other needs. At the time of writing this book, leveraging a financial institution's money can be done at a very low interest rate, far below the rate of return we would receive investing in an investment property, thus making it a no-brainer.

There are a large number of online resources dedicated solely to helping you identify your rate of return with a potential rental property. Going into detail on this topic could be a book of its own, so I encourage you to seek out the resources we have at our fingertips and gain an understanding of calculating cash flow and returns on investment properties if, in fact, you are considering taking your investing and wealth-building plans down this road.

The second reason we opted to leverage a bank's financing rather than buy the investment property in cash, is due to the need to maintain a considerable amount of cash-on-hand in the event we need to make repairs on the existing properties or are faced with an unexpected emergency expense. After all, life happens, and you must be ready. Additionally, we do not want to deplete our cash-on-hand, as that can hinder our ability to use that money to invest in other areas or invest in yet another property.

FAQ: Mortgages are usually fifteen- or thirty-year terms, so how in the world do that many properties get paid off?

While you're venturing out and studying open resources about real estate investing, you may find yourself learning about the "snowball" method of investing in real estate and, subsequently, paying off any/all loans you may have associated with the properties. There is no right or wrong here, and I remind you that this is not a real estate investment guide book. Instead, the key is to have a plan. No two real estate investors' plans will be identical.

For us, we have adjusted our plan over the years as we continue to strategize and modify our short-term goals. However, our long-term goal has remained the same: accumulate enough rental properties to reach financial independence, while concurrently paying down the mortgages to reach a state of debt-free and financial wealth.

What does this really mean? We have put pen to paper and determined how many properties we need to accumulate in order to achieve what we consider for ourselves to be financial independence. For the sake of this example, let's say that number is ten properties. We have done the math and determined that ten properties, once all debt for them has been paid off, will net us $10,000 in monthly cash flow after paying property taxes, insurance, and a forecasted amount of monthly repair expenses.

In addition to determining the number of rental properties we aim to acquire, we have discussed what our current and future goals are regarding the properties. Our end goal is monthly cash flow for use during retirement. As a result, we are not relying upon the rental income to live *today*. This affords us the ability to take every penny of rental income today and apply it toward the next rental property purchase.

This brings us back to the "snowball" method. While it may not be the best method for everyone, it is what we determined is the best for us. We have taken this concept and modified it to fit our goals. Here's how it works: take all of your net rental income and set it aside to be used as a down payment on your next rental property. In doing so, you will be able to purchase each property in a shorter and shorter amount of time as your combined rental income increases (or "snowballs").

When we dipped our toe in real estate investing at the very beginning, we began renting out our first home after finding that we needed to move into a home with more space. Our monthly net rental income on that property was not huge, as we hadn't purchased the property with the intent for it to be an investment with large cash flow. Instead, it was purchased as our first home that we enjoyed for a few years. When we turned it into a rental property, our monthly net rental income was $350.

When Kim and I discovered our knack for real estate investing and decided it would be an integral part of our retirement plans, we began diligently saving money from our careers each month to purchase our second rental property. We also took the $350 net rental income and contributed all of it to that purpose. When the time came that we had saved enough money for a down payment on our second rental property, we found a great deal and went for it! Our total net rental income then became $850, thus allowing us to save enough money for a down payment on rental number three in an even shorter period of time.

We continued purchasing properties one by one and will do so until we have reached our desired number of properties. As you can see, this method will eventually allow you to save a down payment that was largely, if not wholly, saved up using rental income. (In other words, your current tenants gave you the down payment on your next property!) Additionally, let's not forget, your tenants are also paying each one of your mortgage payments!

Ah, yes, mortgage payments, let's not forget about paying down the mortgages so that we will eventually achieve our end goal. In this scenario, we have a deliberate plan in place to pay off the mortgages and ensure we enter retirement debt-free and enjoying that $10,000 of net rental income I mentioned before.

When putting pen to paper, we identified our sweet spot at which point we will stop applying today's rental income toward additional property purchases, and will, instead, apply every penny of net rental income toward paying down the mortgages one by one.

Here is where taking advantage of all those online resources comes into play again. There are numerous mortgage payoff calculators online, and even spreadsheet templates you can download, so that you may input your mortgage details to identify exactly when you are forecasted to pay off a mortgage based on extra payments applied each month. (Seriously, we do this. Kim is obsessed with spreadsheets, and I'm pretty sure her ideal weekend is locking herself in her home office to strategize with new Excel formulas!) When we have stopped (or maybe just paused) buying additional properties, we will begin applying all our net rental income each month to the mortgage on our most-recently acquired property until it is paid off.

For us, we have calculated that that property will be paid off in a period of only two years. Once that property is paid off, our net rental income will have snowballed yet again, and we will apply all that to pay off the next most-recently-acquired property, which, in our case, will be completely paid off in only two years after that. By the time we "retire" at an early age, all our rental properties will be paid off.

Tip: Generally speaking, if your mortgages are all purchased with conventional loans with similar fixed interest rates, paying off your most-recently acquired mortgage first will save you the most money in interest, as mortgages often have most of the interest being paid in the earliest years of the loan.

As I mentioned previously, there is an infinite number of strategies for real estate investing, and my own strategy might be modified as we progress, as well. However, the key is identifying your goals, your risk tolerance, and your financial means to make it happen. Some real estate investors find that buying properties in cash over a longer period of time works best for them. Others use non-traditional financing such as business loans, lines of credit on their primary houses, and so on. Many aggressive investors have found creative financing that allows them to buy a property with $0 out of pocket. No strategy is more right, or more wrong, than another. It comes down to educating yourself with the never-ending supply of resources at our fingertips, and determining if your goal is income *today*, or income in retirement.

MYTH: Investing in real estate is too risky.

Is it, though? Perspective, my friends. I would argue that following a traditional savings plan for retirement carries more risk; a risk of having to pinch pennies during retirement. Let's look at the numbers. 401Ks differ based on the plan, but overall, this investment channel yields a five to eight percent annual return on investment per Melissa Horton at Investopedia. Please don't get me wrong, a 401K is a great savings plan and I am not discouraging any reader of this book from enrolling in a 401K plan, especially if it's employer-matched! Just keep your eyes and ears open for unconventional wealth-building strategies, constantly educate yourself, and know that you do not have to listen solely to advice from others around you.

If you invest in real estate, you WILL be told not to do it. Literally every single person that we told that we were going to rent out our very first home, rather than point out how smart it was or how great it would be to have rental income, they instead told us how risky it was, how someone was going to destroy the home, and how we should really reconsider doing it. While, eventually, those individuals understood what our goal was based on our explanation of our plan, the first reaction from everyone was incredibly negative.

You must decide whether or not you're going to let someone else's opinion dictate your financial future. I can list every success story, ever, in the existence of humanity, and point out something that "could have gone wrong." Part of going into ANY business — real estate or otherwise — is that you have to accept that there will be ups and downs. I have personally never heard of any success story that didn't have the occasional setback or learning opportunity. Will some tenants be better than others? Of course. Will you need to do repairs between tenants? Probably. But that's the cost of doing business.

MYTH: I need to be a real estate agent to invest in real estate.

Definitely not. When Kim and I purchased our first two rental properties, Kim was not a real estate agent. We managed the properties ourselves, as the property owners, because we lived in close proximity. Our only use of a real estate agent was through purchasing the house.

Do you need a good real estate agent to show you houses and help you get a good deal? Absolutely. Do you need to get a real estate license? Not at all. In fact, if you want to purchase properties that were foreclosed upon and are owned by the Housing of Urban Development (HUD), you are better off not getting a real estate license, as real estate agents are not permitted to purchase those types of properties—and there are some great HUD deals you could land! Kim's career as a real estate agent is separate from our real estate investing adventures, and even if she had never obtained her real estate license, we'd still be just as deep in real estate investing as we are now.

Chapter 9: Do People Hate You? Good!

If there's one thing I've learned in the last decade of doing business, it's that people hate to see you winning. It's sad but true. This is an aspect of the human psyche that I will personally never understand, but truly, there is a crazy number of people who love and live to try and break other people down. It's that person(s) who just popped into your head. Yes, you know exactly who I am talking about. It's the person who can't help but point out the negatives before the positives, the person who always lends their critical and usually unhelpful opinion which is often unsolicited, the person who never misses an opportunity to share how they could have done something better, or, my favorite, the person who makes assumptions about you without any basis rooted in fact.

What I have found is that the individuals doing the hating and making the comments are either jealous, struggling with their own issues, projecting their own insecurities and failures onto you, or a combination of all the above.

Kids: My choice. Not Yours.

While this is one of the easiest sections of this book for me to write, it is also one of the most frustrating. My viewpoint and recommendations on this topic are often the hardest for people to understand. If you take only one thing from this chapter, it's to make your decision to have children yours and yours alone, because there WILL be haters surrounding that. Do not make the decision based on what your religion, family or society pushes you toward. If anyone in your life truly cares for you, they will love, support and respect your decision, regardless of the outcome. If they won't, frankly, they don't deserve to be in your life.

My wife and I, years before we were married, made the decision to not have children. It wasn't because we had some strange disdain for children, but rather, we simply did not have the desire to make children part of our future. We followed the advice of this chapter, chose our priorities in life, and saw them through. Far too often, people tend to have kids because it is "what you're supposed to do." I think that belief is one of the biggest crocks of shit our human existence has to offer. We are talking about a human life here. Why would any person willingly want to go down that path when it is not something they truly want? Why put yourself, those around you and the child in question in that position?

Now, admittedly, the path my wife and I chose did not come without frustration and judgment. Most notably, between the ages of eighteen to twenty-six, we were constantly told the following:

"Oh please, you'll change your mind."

"Just wait until she's approaching thirty. Her biological clock will be ticking!"

"Why wouldn't you want to have kids? They're amazing!"

"But we want grandchildren!"

"I want nieces and nephews!"

"But don't you want to give your parents grandchildren?"

"You'll never know what you're missing."

"You two would make such great parents!"

"Don't you want to leave what you've built to someone?"

The list goes on and on. Here's the thing: we don't blame people for asking these questions, no matter how annoying, mainly because we have an unshakable amount confidence in what we want out of life and a solid partnership to back it up. However, that is us. Not everyone has that level of confidence.

I want to be abundantly clear about one thing. If you are a family member or friend, yes, even a parent, who makes comments to their friends or children like those I outlined above, please stop. Not today. Not tomorrow. Now. It often seems as if those who make those comments are projecting their desire for you to live the same life they are, which may or may not be a positive or happy life.

How about if the person you are nagging can't have kids? Guess what? You are now the asshole who is going to make someone incredibly uncomfortable, because now they may feel like they need to divulge information about themselves that is no one's business but that individual and who he or she chooses to share that information with.

Case in point: my wife. Yes, I have received her permission to discuss the following in this book because, well, I enjoy being alive. What only a handful of people know is that my wife suffers from a rare condition called Pseudotumor Cerebri, also known as Idiopathic Intracranial Hypertension (IIH).

IIH is a hell of a condition. It is caused by increased pressure around the brain (with the cause of this pressure being completely unknown by medical professionals). The increased pressure around the brain often mimics the symptoms of a brain tumor without there being an actual tumor. Those symptoms include ringing in the ears, persistent and often severe headaches, changes to vision due to pressure on the optic nerve, light flashes, nausea and dizziness, and shoulder, neck and back pain among others.

Pregnancy, while certainly possible for those with IIH, can add a layer of complexity to the process. To be clear, many women who suffer from IIH have children and there are no issues. One's potential risk for complications is obviously something to be discussed on an individual basis with a physician. Regardless, the key takeaway here is that aside from someone simply not wanting kids, there can very easily be an "invisible" underlying medical issue that is a contributing factor to their decision to not have children. In summary, mind your own business.

Children come with a significant amount of baggage. As mentioned throughout this book, traveling the world, being entrepreneurs and focusing our attention on our careers are what get us out of bed in the morning. For us, adding children to the equation would greatly delay or even completely derail what we want. Many people do all those things while still having children, and I say more power to them. However, again, that isn't what we want. Right about now is when someone would refer to us as being selfish. I can't tell you how many times I have heard this, and each time, it has absolutely zero impact on our decision to live the life we love.

My question back to those individuals, if I cared about their opinion on the topic enough to ask, would be: "What have you done in your life that puts you in a position to judge me?" There would likely be a big swarm of crickets at that moment or a fumbling, bumbling, incoherent answer.

It would be understandable for someone reading this to ask, "But you have built a considerable net worth at such a young age, and you both have great careers, so would having kids really be much of a burden at this point? You have considerable financial resources, so you could still have kids and achieve your dreams." The thing is, conceptually, they wouldn't be wrong. However, again, they're missing one critical variable: it's not what makes us happy — and that, my friends, is what matters.

If you, too, decide to be in the "no kids club," don't be an asshole to those who do have kids, many of whom will likely be your friends and family members. Part of ignoring those who give you a hard time for not having kids is not judging those who decide to start a family. Everyone has their own journey, and you must respect that. Respect their journey not only because it's the decent thing to do, but because you don't want to be like those who give you shit for doing what makes you happy.

So, there's a funny story about my vasectomy. Ha, that's a hell of a transition to a new paragraph, isn't it? Well, this is probably the only place in this book where this story makes sense so, here we go. I mean, I could have dropped it in the real estate or building wealth section to see if you were paying attention, but that's ok. When I made the decision to get a vasectomy, it was an easy one. As already mentioned, we knew we didn't want kids and following my wife's IIH diagnosis, I knew it was snip snip time. Plus, a vasectomy is less invasive compared to a tubal ligation, so for us, we took the lesser of the two recovery times, but that's totally a personal choice. I did the awesome, highly-recommended thing and watched the procedure on YouTube beforehand. I apparently enjoy torturing myself. Yay, me.

The timing of the procedure was quite interesting. I had just resigned from TSYS Merchant Solutions after about six and a half years, and since I was making a career transition to a competitor company, my last day at TSYS was the day I turned in my resignation letter. The next training class at my new employer wasn't for approximately three weeks, so I did two things: first, I booked a trip to Mexico. I mean, when is the last time I had three weeks off work? Second, I went to see my doctor.

Shout out to my doctor, by the way, for not being a judgmental asshat about my age and not having kids. Instead, he gave me the "good for you for knowing what you guys want" line, and we moved on. They had an opening the following Monday, so we put it on the books.

I drove myself to the procedure, as my wife was out closing on a few houses, which I was one-hundred percent ok with. It apparently wasn't going to be a big ordeal. One person was out making money while I was preventing something that would cost us money. Teamwork! Ha!

The time arrived to get the party started. I hopped up on the table, ready to finally cut this worry out of my life. Get it? In the room were a nurse and two doctors. One doctor was younger, and the other was observing. As he was arranging his workspace, the doctor said, "Ok, I'm going to move your ding dong out of the way, and just tape it over here." I don't know what I appreciated more, the use of the term "ding dong" during a medical procedure, or the fact that he so generously insinuated that he had to "move" something out of the way to get started.

I appreciate the boost in confidence, doc. I guess heroes wear lab coats.

The doctor then inquired about my favorite music. My taste in music spans more genres than I can count, but I went with a classic: Metallica. Before I knew it, a Metallica playlist was being streamed into the operating room. As they poked me a few times with a needle and began snipping away, I was whisked away to a happier place by the soothing sounds of "Seek and Destroy," "Harvester of Sorrow," and "Bleeding Me," all appropriately named for the occasion. The downside? Metallica is ruined for me, so that sucks.

As the procedure ended and the final stitches were placed, the doctor said, "Well, Matt, we successfully removed both testicles." A moment of awkward, nervous silence proceeded, followed by a chuckle and the doctor stating, "Haha, I'm kidding. Ah, that's a good one. I say that every time. Never gets old. We're all done here!" It was at this moment that I realized that the doctor was me, had I decided to become a doctor.

Keyboard Warriors

I need to take a deep breath before writing about these "winners." Social media has been one of the most incredible gifts from the technology Gods to have ever graced the reality of human existence. Like most, I am dialed into social media every day, to the point that it might as well be an IV coursing through my veins. I use it for networking, sales, education, inspiration, and entertainment to name a few. I even sprinkle a little ASMR for relaxation (Google it). Social media is truly amazing, as long as it's used for good.

The problem is, it gives the world a level of anonymity—and more concerning, a lack of accountability—that we have never seen before. You can literally say anything, to anyone, at any time, and there are virtually no consequences. Have you ever scrolled down to read the comment section under a post on your favorite social platform? Of course, you have. We all have. Me? Two minutes of scrolling is usually what it takes before my brain explodes.

The comment section under a Facebook post, Instagram photo, Tweet, or YouTube video is the Wild West of the modern era, often filled with disturbing thoughts, horribly inaccurate and unchecked information, strangers dueling as if their lives depended on it, and just overall, well, trash. Seriously, it is mainly heaping piles of wet garbage and dumpster fires.

Are there entertaining responses that make me laugh? Of course, but the prevalence of dumb-dumbs seems to be much more rampant. What cracks me up are the keyboard warriors who you (and everyone else) know would never be able to stand up to those they are trolling if they were to meet in real life. They simply wouldn't. This goes back to this weird phenomenon of people thinking they have magical powers and untold levels of strength and brilliance because they can anonymously spew their verbal diarrhea from the safety of their parents' basement.

Want to know what I do? I block people. I don't spend time scrolling through comments I receive with the goal of finding people to block, but if I do come across a particularly stupid or hateful comment, I simply block them. They could be a friend, family member, acquaintance; it doesn't matter. The block option is fair game in my book (pun intended). Don't be afraid to use it. It can be oddly satisfying.

What's incredibly unfortunate, is the particularly annoying brand of troll who takes the time to try to shoot down people who are doing incredible things in this world and have chosen to share their journey on social media. Trolls post comments without thinking about the immense amount of work and hardship that exists behind the scenes. Much like any other person who has achieved success, the losers of the world are always front and center, ready to project their failures onto you. I think one of the best examples of people who deal with trolls is Casey Neistat.

Casey Neistat is an incredibly talented and inspiring creator with over ten million subscribers on YouTube. I have watched every single video on his channel, and I am one of the millions excited for the next new video notification to pop up. Casey's content covers a wide spectrum of topics from technology reviews, to family life and travel, to entrepreneurship, and everything in between. From my perspective, I get a little bit of everything from his work. What I find inspiring about his background is that he came from nothing.

> "I don't have the time, energy, or interest in hating the haters; I'm too busy loving the lovers."
>
> - Steve Maraboli
> Author: "Unapologetically You: Reflections on Life and the Human Experience"

As Casey has shared many times on his channel, he had a kid in high school, dropped out, lived on floors, and had next to nothing in terms of money or possessions. What he did have was a passion for creating, and the drive to make something of that passion. It's amazing to see someone come from a point that would break most people to the point he is at now. His hustle, risk-taking, and unwavering focus on building something bigger than himself is something that encouraged me to take on many of my entrepreneurial pursuits over the years.

As I've invested the time to watch every video on Casey's channel, I've also scanned through hundreds of comments on his videos. There's one particular video where he addresses haters head-on. The video is appropriately titled, "Dear, Haters." I highly recommend you check it out.

In the video, he refers to comments he has received on his videos that were particularly frustrating to him. He goes on to hold up a piece of cardboard to the camera that read the following quote: "People Who Say It Cannot Be Done Should Not Interrupt Those Who Are Doing It."

I researched who this quote is by and there isn't definitive proof of any one person. Some say Confucius and others say George Bernard Shaw. Who knows? I digress. It really is the perfect anecdote to counter the trolls who spend their time accomplishing absolutely nothing, while the very people who they are trolling are actually out in the world accomplishing the very things they're being told they aren't accomplishing! That's a hell of a stupid thing to deal with.

The reality is that trolls and keyboard warriors aren't going anywhere. They are the modern-day version of the schoolyard bully, but bigger cowards. At least the schoolyard bully had to face people in person. If you are dealing with trolls or any other form of cyberbullying, know that the person behind that keyboard is a loser in the truest sense of the word. While you are focusing on your success, those little shits are settling comfortably into a long life of sadness, struggle, and failure.

Luck, Huh?

Want to bug me? Tell me and my wife how lucky we are. You have no idea how many times we have been, and continue to be, told that we are "just lucky." Just lucky? Get the fuck out of here. Remember, there is a difference between feeling grateful for your opportunities and being told you are just lucky, knowing damn well the person making that comment has absolutely no idea what it took. It reminds me of a quote by Gary Vaynerchuck (Vee) in which he states, "It pisses me off how many people contact me and say how lucky I am 'Oh Gary, you're so lucky'...and I just want to sit there and be like 'Thanks for thinking I'm lucky but remember that time when we were twenty-one and you were at the Jersey shore with hot chicks? I was working my ass off...'"

There are a lot of things Gary Vee says that I think are spot on, but damn, Kim and I can really relate to that quote. I bet many of you reading this can as well.

Consider the following: when we had basically no social life because we worked full-time and went to school full-time at night — was that luck? When I would come home from one job and relentlessly work on my side businesses for the next seven hours, get a few hours of sleep and then do it all over again — was that luck? Early on in Elite Wear, when I was making late night runs to my local post office in the dead of winter at 10:30 p.m. to use the outdoor kiosk to print labels and ship bracelets — was that luck? I can print them at home now, by the way. Ha! How about Kim doing endless days of marketing research and investing her own money, even before making her first sale, in an effort to get her name in front of clients—was that luck? How about meticulously saving and strategically managing our money with the goal of buying an investment property, and another, and another—was that luck?

And how about not just talking about doing big shit, but actually doing big shit—is that luck?

You get my point.

Check Yourself

Despite the title of this chapter—"Do People Hate You? Good!"—it is important to check yourself on occasion to make sure that people aren't hating you because you are truly being an asshole. We are all human, and let's be honest with ourselves. When we start to get a little money, some success, perhaps some notoriety, we start to feel ourselves a bit. It's a natural reaction. I'm not saying everyone who starts to win begins treating other people like peasants, but it's an easy trap to fall into. As I try to do throughout this book, I'll raise my hand.

There was a time when I started to feel myself a bit too much. My net worth was increasing, my title at work carried more weight behind it and people were looking up to me. Damn, I'm pretty awesome, right? Wrong. Thank God I had enough self-awareness to take a step back and think, "Did I really just say that? Did I really just think that? Wait, this isn't me."

You can be successful without being an asshole to people. People are smart enough to see that you're successful because it shows through in your actions, your words, and your results.

I remember being in the car with my parents. Kim and I were sitting in the back. I don't remember where we were going or my exact age, but I was in my early twenties, and I remember we were talking about some of the things Kim and I had accomplished at that point. I started talking about some smart decisions we had made, our dedication to work and investing, and then my dad responded, "So? You want a parade or something? That's what you should be doing." We all laughed, but I was glad he said that because, whether he meant to or not, it reminded me to be humble in my accomplishments and to not think I am special because I'm doing things that a smart, responsible person should be doing anyway.

Success Guilt

I'll admit, this is an interesting topic to follow the previous section, but it's an important one, so I'll do my best to not sound too much like a hypocrite. Don't feel bad that you are successful. I'll say that again, DO NOT feel bad that you are successful. Success guilt is a real thing, and it's something my wife and I have personally discussed on many occasions. We see so many people struggling around us. You know exactly what I'm talking about. We all hear people around us say, "I really need payday to come" or "I literally have no money at the moment" or "I am paycheck to paycheck." Meanwhile, we are over here building an empire.

We have sat up in bed many nights and reflected on how happy we are, while at the same time feeling bad that we don't struggle financially and can really do what we want. In a way, it keeps us humble and ensures that we both recognize how privileged we are to live the life that we do. On the other hand, we've learned that you can keep both feet on the ground while also being proud of yourself for not accepting mediocrity, and instead striving to achieve the incredible.

Success guilt hits me at fairly random moments, usually when I'm winding down and reflecting, but it may be a bigger, more frequent issue for others. So, how can you manage those feelings and stay focused on your goals? How do I manage those feelings? One way to curve success guilt is by giving back. Listen, I've been a long-time believer that no one owes you anything. You have to work for what you want, and never expect handouts. I don't care how rich someone is, I have never in my life looked at that person and felt that they owned me something simply because they have "extra."

Giving Back

Giving back comes in many forms. This book? Frankly, it's a way for me to give back. I've experienced some pretty cool stuff that has helped me learn so much about life and business, and I want others who may not have those same opportunities to draw some level of benefit from my journey.

Do I want it to sell a million copies? Of course, I do! Who wouldn't? However, the idea of someone else improving even a small aspect of their life because of something in this book that spoke to them, well, the possibility of that is what kept me coming back to my phone and computer to keep writing.

How about time? Volunteering your time can be quite powerful, as well. Whether it be with a local animal shelter, homeless shelter, youth center, the list really goes on and on. Just Google the name of your city and Volunteer Opportunities, and you'll be provided with endless options.

One point to make is a critical one and that is to never let society shame you into feeling bad for what you have worked so hard to achieve. Hell, even if you inherited your wealth, again, it doesn't give anyone the right to make you feel bad about who you are or where you're at in life. Self-sabotage is a real thing and something that can get in the way of your success. This is a dangerous symptom of success guilt. I know it sounds silly on the surface, but individuals struggling with success guilt sometimes make the conscious decision to not pursue new opportunities, bring new ideas to the table, or leverage the talents that earned them success in the first place.

Just remember, it's what you choose to do with your success and how you choose to carry yourself that truly matters. I use the word "choose" because it truly is your choice, and as such, you need to be ready for the outcome of that choice.

One way my wife and I give back is through our non-profit, Lily's Lifeline, Inc. Lily's Lifeline was created in the memory of one of our rescued dachshunds, Lily, with the purpose of providing financial assistance to animals and their families when faced with unexpected, critical veterinary expenses. It has been, and continues to be, an incredibly fulfilling venture. What is wonderful about the venture, is that we started it purely out of the genuine desire to give back. Though I am writing this as part of the book that discusses "Success Guilt," I can honestly say that our non-profit came from a place of love and desire to help others.

This book is all about the honest truth, right? As such, I would be remiss if I didn't admit that creating and running a non-profit has indeed curbed many feelings of guilt. Does that make it any less special? Absolutely not. From our perspective, it fills our hearts with an overwhelming feeling of thanks to being in this position.

My wife and I give back where we can, not because we have to, but because we have the genuine desire to do so. We sat down and decided that because we have the means, we should try to have a positive impact on those around us and in our community. Creating a non-profit seemed to be the most organized way of doing so.

While on the topic of non-profits, I always laugh when I hear someone say people only create non-profits as a way to decrease their overall tax bill at the end of the year. I honestly have heard this belief on many occasions. Do people create non-profits for that exact reason in some cases? Of course, they do. Am I mad at them? Nope. If their non-profit is going to have a true, positive and measurably-beneficial impact on others, I personally won't lose sleep because the owner's tax liabilities decreased as a result. Does our non-profit decrease our tax liabilities at the end of the year? Yes, it does, but it's the exact same tax benefit we'd have if we had donated to any other non-profit organization.

Here's what counts: I can honestly say that we would make the contributions we have to this point regardless of whether or not we owned the non-profit.

Chapter 10: My Silent Enemy

Anxiety

Woven into the fabric of the personal and business journey I discuss throughout this book is my struggle with anxiety, something most people don't know about me, not even my family. Anxiety, which is a feeling of worry, nervousness, or unease—typically about an imminent event or something with an uncertain outcome—has long been a silent enemy of mine, stalking me from the bushes, firing shots when I least expect them. Oddly, I often debate how anxiety has helped me. Let's examine that further.

I have a strange relationship with anxiety. I often wonder if I would have excelled in my career so quickly had I not experienced the immense amount of self-inflicted pressure that existed throughout my early to mid-twenties. I say self-inflicted because no one around me ever pressured me to be anything specific in life.

It sounds strange to write down that thought, as I know many others have terrible outcomes related to their anxiety. But as it relates to my journey, it's something I often ponder. As mentioned, many reading this will be quite surprised at my "admission," because I simply don't talk about it outside of my wife or therapist, and most people can relate with a justified or unjustified fear that waving the flag of mental health can result in negative judgment against you.

Now at age thirty-one, anxiety, while still like that annoying "friend" who only shows up when they need something, plays a much smaller role in my life. I'm at a place now that simply isn't surrounded by stress or constant pressure. Sure, a reasonable amount of stress exists in my professional life, but that comes with the territory of being a director in corporate America with ambitions of one day becoming a VP and beyond. My family is proud of me and all that I have accomplished, a fact that I know I have never questioned once in my life. I have been surrounded by, and continue to surround myself with, leaders of industry and those who build you up to be the best version of you.

If I have learned anything on the topic of anxiety and stress management, it's that you aren't weak by seeking help to work through your issue(s). In fact, you are quite the opposite. It takes a strong person to look in the mirror and admit that they are struggling, and an even stronger person to make the conscious decision to meet with a professional. You aren't crazy, and you aren't a failure. Frankly, you're a much stronger person than those who live in fear of being judged by others as a result of seeking help, despite the fact that no one would find out unless you told someone... or mentioned it in a book you're writing for the world to read.

A State of Ignorance

There are many topics in our society that are littered with unfathomable amounts of misinformation and ignorance. I've discussed money being one of those topics, and another is mental health.

I won't turn this book into a politically-driven manuscript on why our society sucks in so many aspects, but the stigma around mental health is one that must be eradicated. I went years without seeking help purely because according to society if I met with a counselor, therapist, nurse, or any other mental health professional, I was suddenly an unstable person with a laundry list of issues. How stupid is that?

The term "mental health" encompasses more topics than I could ever list, and we, as a society, need to work toward removing the associated stigma. I think we would all be surprised at how much happier we would be as a society. You want to talk about irony? There is a long list of people who have continually fed the negative stigma around anxiety and other forms of mental health yet have continually reached out to me and people like me for business and money advice. Imagine the thoughts that will go through their heads when they learn that the guy who apparently holds a bunch of magical advice and knowledge has struggled with anxiety for the last sixteen years. I get some sort of strange joy out of that thought.

If you are reading this book, and either know someone or think you might have an issue with anxiety but are either too embarrassed or scared to seek treatment, consider the following facts:

- Anxiety is the most common mental health disorder in the U.S., affecting close to forty million adults [10]. That's over eighteen percent of the U.S. population.

- Despite such a staggering number, only about one-third of those who struggle with anxiety receive treatment [10]. This is likely due to the stigma surrounding mental health.

Think about those statistics for a minute.

What's ironic is the level of anxiety I have about talking about my issues with anxiety. Ain't that some shit?

One way I dealt with my anxiety, was by working more. A lot more! I know that sounds strange, but everyone copes differently. Since my anxiety was rooted in self-doubt and worry that I was wasn't achieving enough in corporate America, my response was to work longer hours and become further lost in my work. The promotions and money further reinforced my bad habits.

Don't shed any tears for me, though. No violins. You won't hear me complain about promotions or more money. It's what I wanted, and I'm glad it happened. My point is that, instead of learning to manage my work constructively, I just doubled down and fed the monster. The monster is still around, by the way. I just manage him instead of the other way around.

I used to read my corporate career emails obsessively. Seriously, I would not only read my emails over and over again before I sent them, but I would read, and reread emails people sent to me, picking apart each word. I was so inside my own head thinking about how my email would be interpreted, or how I should interpret an email from a coworker, that it started to become counterproductive. I would be working on my laptop late at night and my wife would say, "Are you reading the same email over and over again?" Damnit! I was!

The most challenging part of dealing with anxiety early on was the long nights. Night after night, I would lay in bed. My wife and dogs were sound asleep, but my eyes and mind were still wide open. I knew that when night would fall, my journey into a dark, endless tunnel would begin. In my mind would be the day's events on an endless, vivid loop. I would examine everything, including the day's events, my words, my emails and conversations I had with colleagues. My stomach would be in knots thinking about everything I could have done better, what people around me could have done better, what people think of me, and the challenges that would inevitably come the following day. I would create scenario after scenario in my mind of what would happen, some of which had merit, but most did not.

This went on for years. One of the reasons I used to work so late into the night was because I knew that going to bed would be pointless, and I might as well be productive. I did not learn or realize until I was in therapy that this filling of my sleep time with work time only worsened my anxiety. "Anxiety causes sleeping problems, and new research suggests sleep deprivation can cause an anxiety disorder. [11]" Sounds exhausting, right? Well, it is.

Therapy helped me understand that it was okay to shut off my "traditional work," and redirect my thoughts to other passion projects. Hello, music! Hello, Elite Wear! Hello, Photography! Hello, Drones! My therapist never told me to not work as hard, but instead, manage my many interests in a more constructive way.

I started to pick times to step away from my career job and focus on my side projects, all of which were often very therapeutic. Seriously, making a bracelet can be quite calming. Oh, and that important sleep thing.

There are a lot of important thoughts and tips throughout this book. Money, business, entrepreneurship, it's all awesome stuff that can change your life. What you MUST NOT IGNORE, is the importance of managing your mental health. STOP being embarrassed to seek treatment. Therapy is a beautiful thing! Your leg hurts, you go to a doctor. You break a finger, you go to a doctor. Yet, the sleepless nights and constant worry that can often be debilitating continues to be ignored.

Are you a kid? Talk to your parents. Are you a parent? Talk to your kid, and don't shut them down when they say they want to speak with a therapist. Have a spouse? Talk to him or her! If your own spouse can't be supportive of your meeting with a therapist, you need to seriously reconsider that relationship, because if anyone should be your one-hundred percent support system, it's your spouse.

Another revelation from therapy was that I can't expect those around me at work to want the same things I want. I used to get so frustrated, especially in my early- to mid-twenties, when those who worked for me or around me weren't putting in the hours I was. What I failed to realize is that not everyone wants the life I want.

As a manager of people, I had to realize that I couldn't expect everyone to be ok with logging on from home at 10:00 p.m. at a moment's notice. My bosses loved that about me, of course, and I'm sure my level of flexibility and dependability played a part in my promotions, but that doesn't mean that path is for everyone.

Hell, there were a number of years early on where I wouldn't take time off. That probably didn't help my anxiety at all. In fact, I know now that it made it worse. Funny enough, I have always been flexible with allowing and encouraging those who work for me to take time off, but I was always bad about following my own advice on that topic. I have learned over the years to take advantage of the time off I do have so that I can be as fresh as possible while in the office. That's the same attitude I want from my employees.

Take your damn vacation so you can be the best of the best while at work! I honestly can't think of a time in the last five to seven years that I actually declined someone's vacation. Seriously people, don't give back vacation time to your employer. It's there for a reason!

Admittedly, before I came to terms with the fact that I needed to talk to a professional to better understand my state of mind, I, too, fed the monster of ignorance around mental health in the United States. I would find myself thinking, "Mental health? That's an issue for crazy people. Why should I care about mental health?"

Be honest with yourself, if someone were to ask you right now to define mental health, could you confidently answer them? Most likely not, but don't feel bad. You are a member of a very large club—one that needs to drastically shrink—and there's only one way this can happen: education.

Anxiety Knows No Age Boundaries

My hope is that the readers of this book span a wide range of age groups. One main reason is that I want to help remove the stigma of anxiety and mental health at all levels, regardless of your phase in life. One thing is certain, and that is anxiety knows no age boundaries. It doesn't care who you are or what generation you're from. "A survey of over 1,000 U.S. adults by the American Psychiatric Association (APA) found that anxious feelings increased the most over the past year among baby boomers (between fifty-four and seventy-two years of age) in comparison to Generation Zers (thirty-eight to fifty-three), and millennials (twenty to thirty-seven). However, Millennials continued to be the most anxious overall. [12]"

The study goes on to measure five categories and their impact on the participant's anxiety: health, safety, finances, relationships, and politics. Unsurprisingly, "Americans were found to be more anxious in all five criteria but being able to pay bills caused the most stress. Almost three quarters of women and millennials, and nearly four in five Hispanic respondents said they felt somewhat or extremely anxious about paying their bills. [12]"

"The poll also offered insight into how Americans perceive mental health and stigma. Despite half of the respondents saying there is less stigma against people with mental illness, they admitted they would not vote for a candidate for public office who had been diagnosed with a mental illness—even if they received treatment. [12]" Well, I am not running for office, but you are reading my book. Does my struggle with anxiety make my achievements and REAL results any less important or inspiring to you? You decide.

My anxiety and the related symptoms have varied in severity over the years. I've experienced everything from feeling mildly sick to my stomach, to more extremes such as having full on panic attacks, and everything in between. Not being able to catch my breath, sweating, the room spinning, and having to literally drop to my hands and knees to stop from falling over have all been my unfortunate partners in this crappy dance that is anxiety.

Even in the face of this thing I will deal with for the rest of my life, I consider myself fortunate. Many who experience anxiety have notably more severe symptoms like depression, addiction, and even suicide. For some, anxiety itself is just one part of a larger, even more difficult type of mental illness — perhaps social anxiety, panic disorder, post-traumatic stress disorder (PTSD), agoraphobia, and more [13]. I have been fortunate enough to not experience any of the aforementioned, but that doesn't make my symptoms (or yours) any less or more important. Dealing with anxiety and any other form of mental health issue is a very personal journey and one that must be managed in your own way.

Perspective

I remember quite vividly my dad coming in my room the morning before a deployment to Iraq in the mid-2000s. I was still in high school at the time. He came in to give me a hug and tell me he loved me. I cannot even begin to imagine what was going through his head, but from my perspective, I was sad, scared, and honestly felt that the brief moment we shared that morning could very well have been the last. It was a pretty awful feeling and one that is still hard to stomach, even today. You don't really know what to say in those situations, especially as a teenager. The gravity of life and death hasn't truly entered into your frame of mind at that point. At least, I hope not.

Today, I know that he knows that he would never have to worry about my mom if something were to happen to him. I only wish I could have been then where I am in life now so that I could ease any worry he had about the well-being of my mom and my family. Well, I can say now that if anything were to happen to him, he would never have to worry about my mom. Mom, I know you're reading this. I got you, Madre.

In the years to come, he would deploy a number of times between Iraq and Afghanistan, some deployments more eventful than others. There would be attempts on his life more than once, something I knew could happen but was taken aback when learning that it actually took place. From vehicle born improvised explosive devices to snipers, the enemy tried, but they failed.

As a young man in the safety of his home back in the States, hearing these stories that involve your own dad simply boggled the mind. The benefit of my father being of higher rank and in a command position is that he often had a Protective Security Detail or PSD when he would move from point A to point B. I truly hope the members of his various PSD's over the years recognize the weight that was removed from mine and my family's shoulders, knowing that our father was in good hands. If any of you are reading this book, on behalf of my entire family, we thank you. If we ever meet, drinks are most definitely on me.

As I've operated in business over the years, I've often been asked why I don't freak out about things or get too overly upset when something happens. Emotional Intelligence? Definitely, but that's not all. Don't get me wrong, I get concerned when things fail, or someone reporting to me makes a poor decision or a client is angry about an issue, and I address it accordingly. I don't minimize those situations or give them any less of my attention. However, if anything, these stories, and the experiences of war my father has shared with me has taught me to put things in perspective.

I am not dealing in life or death on a daily basis. No one is trying to kill me. At least, I hope not. I am a decent manager, I promise. Ha! No one is going to die because a client is upset about an issue. I remember one night in my early twenties sitting in my car outside of a grocery store in the dead of winter. My fiancé at the time and I had just picked up a few items for the coming weekend. This was during the years when my parents were helping pay for my college. I remember telling my parents that, while I appreciate them helping, I don't want to be a financial burden as I would prefer that they focus on retirement and not on me.

If you recall from earlier in this book, I was contributing hundreds of dollars per month to my education to lessen their burden, but despite that, I still felt a tremendous amount of guilt. My dad said something that stuck with me and transformed the way I look at many situations. He said, "Matt, we have the ability to help, and, more importantly, we want to help. When you spend a year dealing with people trying to kill you and those around you, money becomes a whole hell of a lot less important."

One way that I have been able to effectively manage my anxiety, is to think back to that conversation with my parents. Even though the topic at hand was about money, for me, the greater lesson out of that conversation is that not everything in life carries with it the same level of importance. One of my biggest struggles with anxiety, especially early on, was that I treated everything as if it was the absolute most important thing going on in my life. Over time and through therapy, I have learned to mentally prioritize the things that truly matter to me.

Chapter 11: The Money Mindset

There's Enough to Go Around

There is a lot of money to be made in this world. People often get lost in the "wealthy own the majority of the money" sad song, and although that fact is true, do you realize how much money is available for the taking? I have never once sat back and complained that I don't have X amount of dollars because the top one percent of the country controls the majority of the wealth, yet I hear people make this very complaint. Instead, I sit up in my chair and put my brain to work to figure out how I, too, can tap into the vast ocean of money that exists in our world.

Now, I would be remiss if I didn't share my opinion about one aspect of top-level executive compensation that I don't agree with. I am one-hundred percent for bonuses. Bonuses don't bother me at all, even when they are astronomically high figures. Honestly, I think it's awesome, motivating, and I hope to be at that level one day.

Think about it. You worked your ass off to get to that level, you carry a tremendous amount of weight on your shoulders, and in many cases, the company you lead thrives or dies based on many of your words and actions. What I don't agree with is receiving gigantic bonuses when your company is not performing. If your company's stock price is tanking, you are laying off employees left and right, locations are being closed, and your brand's reputation is being dragged through the mud, how do the top-level leaders of that organization deserve massive bonuses?

I understand employment contracts enough to know that those payouts are often tied to retention clauses and other incentives aimed at keeping the top-level talent on board, through good times and bad. However, the same question remains. Something to ponder.

Moving on, if you are someone whose productivity or ability to tap into the river of money that flows around us continually fails because you are so bitter and preoccupied will the many aspects of our society that seem upside down, I encourage you to re-evaluate. You don't have to agree with how large corporations operate or how professional athletes make more money than most people but are you going to allow your jealousy and disdain for those individuals to influence your mindset to the point that you don't achieve extraordinary financial results of your own? That seems like a tremendous waste of a life.

I have worked for several different companies over the last ten-plus years, and they weren't always the most successful, but that didn't mean *I* couldn't be successful. Are you noticing a theme in these last few paragraphs? Focusing on what you can control is everything.

When I was nineteen, I worked for a company that went through a very controversial time. The founder and CEO were in a battle against the board of directors and were ultimately forced out. The company was plagued with frequent layoffs. The ownership of the company changed hands more than once, and with those changes came new CEOs with new visions and new directions. Not to mention, the recession of 2008 was in full swing.

As you can imagine, the worry in the air at the office was palpable. I would hear people make comments about the executives, how much money they make, the new CEO, how no one cares about the employees, and so on. I could have kept my head down, engaged in negative conversations about our leaders, or distracted myself and others with fear-mongering. Did I? Hell no. I accepted that some things I cannot control, and bitching about it would add exactly zero value to anything.

Instead, I turned my focus to what I could control, and the results that focus yielded were very positive. I earned production bonuses, started training new employees, and gave presentations to large crowds including executives. I moved from an individual contributor role to a supervisor and gained some of the most valued experience I could have hoped for at that point in my young career.

There is a lot about this world that is wrong. That is no secret. I try to impact what I can in the most positive way possible, and that will never change. I am human, and I get frustrated when I see certain companies make a decision I don't agree with, or our government continuing to make an ass out of itself on a daily basis. But is that going to distract me to a point that I never achieve something extraordinary? Hell no. If you are someone who is constantly caught up in things outside of your control and also wondering why you aren't advancing in your career, your business, and your bank account, it's time to shut off the noise, stop complaining, focus on what you are good at and get to work. Your future self will thank you.

Money Doesn't Remove Passion

One type of person who I have always admired but many don't seem to understand, are those who continue to work after they've achieved extraordinary financial success. Continuing to work when you have enough money to stop is often viewed by some as greedy, money hungry, blah blah blah. I chuckle when I hear people make those comments because they clearly don't understand the love of the hustle, and most likely would love to quit whatever it is they are doing the first chance they get.

You know the names:

Warren Buffet: $80B Net Worth

Bill Gates: $90B Net Worth

Elon Musk: $22B Net Worth

Jay Z: $900M Net Worth

Jeff Bezos: $112B Net Worth

Mark Zuckerberg: $53B Net Worth

The list goes on...

What so many fail to understand is that the money these individuals have amassed came from the love of their respective fields, and that love is incredibly difficult to break up with. There's a quote: "Do what you love, and you'll never work a day in your life." I believe this could be applied to the aforementioned group and many others. Just because you reach a certain financial milestone, doesn't mean that your creativity, your love for negotiating deals, or your love for going to the office and grinding magically disappears.

The first time my wife and I made over $500,000 in a year, honestly, didn't feel any different from any other year. We, of course, took a step back for a second, laughed with excitement that we had reached that milestone, shit our pants at the amount we paid in taxes (no violins, please. We know it's a first world problem). But then that all quickly passed, and we got back to work.

I didn't buy a Lamborghini, we didn't go on a Gucci shopping spree, and I didn't buy that Rolex I've been looking at for ten years. We went to bed in the same house we built in 2012 for $258,500, and we tackled the next day with the same level of passion we had when we lived in a $725 per month one-bedroom apartment and had a household income of $50,000 a decade earlier. You read that right, by the way. $50,000 to $500,000+ in just under 10 years. There's no reason you can't do the same.

All the individuals listed above have incredible stories of how they built their companies, their ups and downs, and the astronomical levels of wealth they have amassed, but there's one in particular I want to expand on: Elon Musk. His story has been told a million times, but I'll hit the points that are most inspiring and will hopefully spark something in you as they did in me. For those who don't know of Elon Musk, he runs Tesla Motors and SpaceX. In 2019, if you haven't heard of those two companies, well, you must live in a tent in the woods.

What's most inspiring to me about Elon is that he worked some pretty tough gigs before becoming the Elon we all know today. According to Ashlee Vance's biography on him, he worked a number of odd jobs, and eventually accepted a job via the unemployment office as a boiler room cleaner at a lumber mill [14]. "The grueling work involved wearing a hazmat suit, crawling through small spaces, and shoveling residue in extremely high-temperature conditions, according to Musk. [14]"

He went on to become a summer intern at the Bank of Nova Scotia making $14 an hour while attending college. I talk a lot about the power of the side hustle in this book. As a way to earn extra money, Musk sold computer parts and fixed people's computers out of his dorm. At one point, after transferring to a different university, he turned his house into a nightclub, using the proceeds to pay his rent.

He eventually moved away from formal education and decided to leverage the internet to power his next move. Along with his brother, they started a company called Zip2, a company that provided directories and maps to newspapers online. Zip2 was eventually purchased in 1999 by a computer company, Compaq, making Musk a none-too-shabby $22M [14].

Let's stop right here for a moment. $22M is an insane amount of money. Hell, you could pay yourself $225,000 per year for the next eighty years and just hang out living a pretty comfortable life. Did Elon Musk? Ha, what do you think?

He took $12 million, yes, that's right, $12 million of his own money, and invested it in a company called X.com. Elon's vision of X.com was for it to become the future of online banking. In the year 2000, X.com merged with its rival, Confinity. As part of that merger, the entity was renamed... drum roll, please... PayPal. That's right. PayPal. The platform that is still going strong at the time of writing this book, and I personally use for all my businesses. It gets even crazier from here.

Get this: Elon was ousted as CEO from PayPal due to internal disagreement, but was still the majority shareholder in the company. PayPal, against Elon's advice, was sold to eBay in 2002. Elon's proceeds from the deal? $180 million. Did Elon call it a day and sail away with his boatload of cash? What do you think? Negative! Passion wins again!

In 2003, he invested a huge amount of those proceeds into starting two companies, SpaceX and Tesla, both of which would continue to require capital investment from his own pocket. As he freely admits on many occasions, both companies almost went bankrupt in 2008.

"I gave both SpaceX and Tesla a probability of less than ten percent likely to succeed," Elon told a crowd at a South by South West (SXSW) conference [15]. He went through a divorce around that same time and, as he shared with that same crowd, he "had to borrow money from his friends to pay his rent. [15]" Fast forward to 2019, we all know the massively successful outcomes of both SpaceX and Tesla. If we know anything about Elon Musk, what those two companies will achieve in the coming years will continue to change our lives, here on Earth and beyond.

By the way, fun fact for those who love to hate executives for their compensation: ss announced by Tesla in January 2018, "Tesla chief Elon Musk will forgo all compensation if the company does not reach milestones regarding valuation and operations. Elon will receive no guaranteed compensation of any kind — no salary, no cash bonuses, and no equity that vests simply by the passage of time. Instead, Elon's only compensation will be a one-hundred percent at-risk performance award, which ensures that he will be compensated only if Tesla and all of its shareholders do extraordinarily well. [16]"

Our level of wealth is obviously not even in the same galaxy as Elon Musk, but on a smaller scale, my wife and I are following a similar path in terms of investing our profits in what we care about. When we make more money, instead of stepping back, we press forward. We take calculated risks and put our profits to work. Having a passion for something and enjoying the daily grind is more powerful than any dollar amount. Passion gives you purpose, and if you are adding value, or in Elon's case, changing the world for the better, money will follow.

Are You Willing?

This life isn't for everyone, and you must ask yourself if you're willing to put in the time and do what it takes. The road I have traveled, which is far from over, is paved with discipline, long hours, stress, and decisions that could crush most. It's also beyond fun. That fun far outweighs what most people would consider negative.

Let me tell you about my routines. I wake up at 6:30 a.m. and head to my job in corporate America. On my way, I make my daily stop to the drive-through mail drop off at my local post office to ship the stack of bracelet orders I packaged the night before. I get to the parking lot of my job around 7:20 a.m., and for the next fifteen minutes, I post some content on my various business social media platforms, respond to client comments or emails, then I head in.

Assuming I've reached an appropriate point in my work to call it a day, I usually head home between 5:00-6:00 p.m.. By 6:45 p.m., I am in my home office working on making new bracelet designs, photographing and editing product photos, updating the Elite Wear and Etsy shops, completing new bracelet orders, editing drone videos from Get It Sold Drone Services, and editing photos from Aspects & Angles Photography. It doesn't stop there.

I work on designing new pillows for Just Throw It Pillows (a company my wife and I launched at the end of 2018), and update the website and Etsy store. I also spend time adding photos to three to five stock photography websites, something I started in 2018 and is slowly starting to take off. I continue working on the aforementioned items until around 10:30 p.m. at which time I head to bed.

While in bed, I would post a few more photos on social media, write a few paragraphs for this book, and begin thinking about the next day. I finally fall asleep around 11:30 p.m. most nights, and then do it all over again the next day. That's what it takes.

My wife's daily routine is on another level. Let's start with money. When it comes to money, we are partners and our planning and any other general discussion around money takes place as a single unit. However, I will gladly and proudly call Kim the CFO. Let me tell you about her spreadsheets. Since our days in the one-bedroom apartment, Kim has been tracking our income, savings, investments, and other data in Excel. No, seriously, she makes it a part of her routine to review our finances every single morning while she's having her cup of coffee and she has done this nearly every morning since we were eighteen.

As time went on, her spreadsheets evolved into masterfully-detailed projections including the amount we needed to make each month and year to reach our goals; of which were mapped out for more than five years into the future. This investment in time and analytics gives us a clear, mutual understanding of what our money is doing, and it ensures that we are positioning ourselves to build considerable wealth.

There have been many weekends where Kim has said, "Hey, I want to stay in and look at our money in a few new ways I've been thinking about. I think we can pay off these five investment properties over here sooner than we thought if we do X, Y, Z and save X, Y, Z by doing so. I want to do the math and then we can review together."

I can, without hesitation, say that this level of tracking and understanding of our financial life contributed greatly to our current net worth. Understanding your own financial health is truly integral to building a healthy financial future.

Chapter 12: Time to Choose

Well, my friends, here we are. At this point, you have read my stories and considered my advice. You know how I feel about a host of societal trends and topics. And you have, most importantly, learned about the REAL results achieved that backup everything I have shared. There are no gimmicks here, no get rich quick schemes, no bullshit.

Where do you go from here? Making that critical "fork in the road" decision is really the point in all of this where most people fail. They get excited after reading a book or hearing someone speak, and they are filled with thoughts of wonder and possibility, but then... nothing.

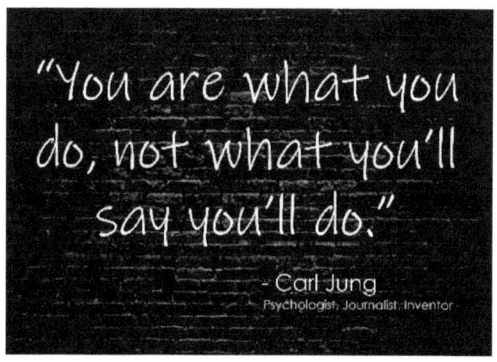

There's the saying, "Everyone wants to be a boss until it's time to do boss shit." If you are truly ready to change your life and achieve extraordinary results, you will start NOW. While your next steps may differ based on your current stage in life, the critical component embedded in all this that doesn't and will never change is one word: ACTION.

While writing this book, I have done a tremendous amount of reflection, and the two overarching themes I always seem to come back to are Mindset and Choices. You must choose to have a winning mindset, and then use that mindset to make winning choices.

You can have the most positive mindset in the world, but if you continually self-sabotage by hanging out with losers, allowing societal norms to dictate your decisions, feeding into the visceral tub of shit that is the comment section on social media, and failing to grab your life by the throat and own it, you will never win. You will live a life of mediocrity, a life of constant struggle, a life filled with regret. And then what? You die. You will have squandered this amazing opportunity that being a human has afforded all of us.

> "The single most powerful asset we all have is our mind. If it is trained well, it can create enormous wealth in what seems to be an instant."
> - Robert T. Kiyosaki
> Author: "Rich Dad, Poor Dad"

The way you decide to view money will be a major driver of the type of life you will have. You can view money as this evil thing that represents nothing but greed and sadness in your life, or you can view it like I do: a tool that can be leveraged to build businesses, provide a valuable service, create passive income, and enables me to give back to those in need.

There's this misplaced notion that money doesn't matter. You're welcome to believe that. I will never believe that. You want to send your kids to private school? Money. You want to travel to Europe to see the ancient ruins in Greece? Money. You want to make a monetary donation to your local animal shelter? Money. You want to give the gift of a formal college education to your kid? Money.

You aren't a bad person for placing a high priority on money. From my perspective, if I haven't already made it abundantly clear, you're a hell of a lot smarter than most people in the room if you understand the value of money and how it can be leveraged to change your life and the lives of those around you. If you waste your energy judging those with money, saying that society is stupid for rewarding highly-compensated people, and endlessly rant about how the world is out to get you, maybe this extraordinary life just isn't for you. You must make that decision for yourself.

However, I can promise you one thing: those people living the incredible lives, hustling their asses off every day, putting in the work and being rewarded handsomely, well, they aren't thinking about you.

You must decide what type of life you want to live. You could be a family of four making $60,000 a year, never take work home with you, live in a modest house, and get by with little stress and be the happiest, most content person on Earth. That's amazing, and if that is what you want from this life, no one is happier for you than me.

Conversely, you could have $50,000,000 in the bank and be miserable, or also the happiest, most content person on Earth. My choice? Find value in taking full advantage of every waking second in this life to build an empire and make a lot of money along the way.

Money equals freedom. Again, MONEY EQUALS FREEDOM. Freedom to choose. Freedom to positively impact others. Freedom to do whatever the fuck you want in life.

Money allows me to not worry about bills, where my next meal will come from, where I'm going to live, and other necessities. Instead, money allows me to travel the world, to gain new perspectives on life, and to take an idea in my head and bring it to life almost immediately.

One of the most incredible feelings in the world to me is thinking of an idea for a product or service and just making it happen. Generally, that takes money. Maybe not a lot but some. If it fails, that's ok. I'll learn from it and move on. I have the option to not worry about failing, and instead focus my attention on learning! The freedom of having options is everything, and it makes the daily grind beyond worth it. If people around you can't accept that or understand it, they just aren't meant to play in your world.

You own your destiny. No one else. Blaming the world for your shortcomings is the fastest way to lose at this game called life. Whatever path you choose, be ready to accept and own the type of life that comes with that choice. I often see people who fancied themselves "too badass" for everyone and everything. You know the type. We all do. They were so worried about being cool in high school, putting on a front to seem like they didn't care about anything.

Now I see those people walking alongside the road in all their "badassery" with no car or no driver's license, but still walking with some badass swagger cuz they coo, yo. Thirty going on twelve. Yeah, you enjoy that. We all know a family member or friend who complains about their current station in life and how unhappy they are. Have they ever considered the choices THEY MADE to get them to that point of unhappiness? If you were to put that person's life on paper for, say, the last ten years, it'd likely be easy to say, "Ah ha, well, here's why..."

How about the life of an entrepreneur? Not just someone who says they're an entrepreneur because it's a popular buzz word, but truly the individual who embraces the long days, long nights, calculated risks, the good times, the hard times, the judgment, the hate, all because they know they are working toward greatness.

It is a lonely path at times, but damn, those hard years are beyond worth it when you've finally reached the point that you're sitting on a beach planning your sunset stroll in the surf instead of stressing about the bullshit the rest of the world is dealing with.

What you put out into this world matters. Be a positive influence to those around you. Whether you recognize it or not, if you are doing anything positive in this life, there is someone watching, studying your moves, trying to understand how you do what you do. Hell, you can probably guess by some of the quotes in this book who I choose to look up to. The possibility of another human choosing to make you the example they want to follow is an incredible honor.

I want you to really think about that. It is a privilege to have even one person follow you, admire what you do, and want to borrow key pieces of knowledge and hustle from your example to then build their own extraordinary life. No matter how much success you have at the time of reading this book or where you end up twenty years from now, there is an endless amount of value to add to every single person you come in contact with. This life is a gift. This life is an opportunity. What you choose to do with it from here is what truly matters.

Stop Listening.

Take Action.

Achieve the Extraordinary.

Acknowledgments

Kim: You are my partner in life and business. Everything we have experienced has been as an unbreakable team. Everything we have, we have built together. You inspire me every day with your passion for business, and for always pushing us to be and do better. No matter what idea I have, you always provide your unwavering support and encouragement, and for that, I am forever grateful. You also do a great job of bringing me back down to earth when I need it. I wouldn't want to be on this journey with anyone else. You are also the best dog/cat mom in human existence. They are the only living creatures luckier than me!

Mom and Dad: Being able to say that I am your son will forever be one of my greatest sources of pride in life. You both have done an indescribable amount for our family, our country, and countless others. Your selfless dedication to service, unmatched adaptability and humble approach to servant leadership is beyond inspiring, and if I have even a fraction of the positive impact you have had on those around you, I will consider my life a success. I love and appreciate you both more than you'll ever know.

Grandparents, Aunts & Uncles: You have all supported and encouraged me in countless ways over the years. You each made my childhood awesome, filled with adventure and constant entertainment. You are all successful in your own ways, and I am thankful to have had you to look up to as role models, especially in the area of work ethic. I carry that work ethic with me always.

Vera Woodson: Vera "Woody" Woodson, you are actually the only teacher from childhood who I have stayed in contact with. I remember reaching out to you back in 2007, about a year after graduating from WSHS, with questions and feedback on a few business ideas I was working on. Over the years, you have always been a great source of encouragement. You are always gracious with your time and wisdom, and for that, I am eternally grateful. Also, thank you for choosing to mold the minds of the future. Having teachers like you in our education system makes me confident that we will have productive, value-adding future members of our society.

Gilberto "Tito" Guzman: My best friend! We have had some crazy times over the years, and no matter what, from junior high to now, you have always been a text or call away, no matter where life has taken us. Even when we both get busy, we always pick up right where we left off. Regardless of the topic, you have always been a consistent presence in my life and, most importantly, a friend. I'm beyond thankful for you, brother.

My Teams: To the many teams I have managed over the last thirteen years, it has been, and continues to be, a personal honor and privilege. You taught me so much about myself and, most importantly, how to be a leader. It is not easy to put your trust and confidence in someone to lead you through both stormy seas and blue skies, and although I didn't always have the answers (and still don't), you stuck by my side, challenged me, and pushed through to success. Seeing you grow, succeed and accomplish your goals is what gets me out of bed every morning. I genuinely believe that any success I have enjoyed in business would not have been possible without you. I am so incredibly proud of all of you, and I look forward to our many journeys to come.

My Leadership: I have been beyond fortunate to have leaders above me who guided me over the years, but also allowed me to make mistakes, learn from them, and grow as a person and professional. You have all been sources of inspiration and education, helping me navigate the many challenges that come with leading people. There isn't a day that goes by where I don't apply something you have taught me. You all know who you are.

My Customers: It is never lost on me that anyone can be put out of business simply by your customers choosing to spend their hard-earned money with your competitors. The fact that you have continuously come back to me — whether it be with Elite Wear, Aspects & Angles Photography, Get It Sold Drone Services, or Just Throw It Pillows — remains one of the most humbling aspects of my life. Your support has allowed me to live my dreams in many regards, and aside from providing a quality service and product, one thing I can promise you is that I will never take your support for granted. Thank you!

About the Author

Matthew Bills has lived an interesting life in his short thirty-one years. Recognizing and being thankful for the incredible opportunities he has had along the way, he was inspired to share his experiences with the sincere hope that even one person would use his experiences to improve their own position in life. Matthew currently serves as Director of Client Services at a leading payments company. In this role, he leads a team of Fraud Strategists responsible for protecting a portfolio of financial institutions and millions of cardholders from potential fraud. Prior to his current role, Matthew served as Director of Client Services at TSYS Merchant Solutions, where he had operational responsibility for customer service, national account support, merchant boarding, merchant deployment, merchant training, and independent sales organization (ISO) support.

It was during his tenure at TSYS Merchant Solutions where he became one of the youngest individuals in the company's over thirty-five-year history to be promoted to Associate Director at age twenty-five, followed by Director at twenty-seven.

Matthew has never been one to waste time outside of his traditional career, but rather finds a great deal of pleasure investing that time in other ventures. A self-taught musician since the age of twelve, Matthew started a music production company, Right Beat Productions, during his senior year of high school at the age of seventeen, producing instrumentals or "beats" for rappers and vocalists all over the world.

In 2015, he started the affordable luxury bracelet company, Elite Wear. By the end of 2018, the company had sold thousands of bracelets. Elite Wear has clients in fifty countries around the world, a retail reseller in Italy, and a following of over 25,000 on Instagram—a group he proudly refers to as "Elite Wear Family Members." Matthew is an avid FAA-certified drone pilot, and in 2017, he started Get It Sold Drone Services, a company that provides unique aerial videography and photography for real estate agents and business owners in Omaha, Nebraska and surrounding cities. This is in addition to a more traditional photography company he launched in 2018, called Aspects & Angles Photography.

Today, Matthew, along with his wife—real estate superstar Kim Bills—owns and operates Crucero Properties, LLC. Together, they purchase condos and single-family homes, add modern updates, and then offer them as rental housing units. As of 2019, they own eight properties with plans of acquiring at least five more over the next ten years.

Matthew will be the first to credit his parents, Mike and Megan, for providing both an unorthodox and supportive upbringing. Matt's father, at the time of writing this book, is an active duty army Lieutenant General and has served for thirty-seven years, three of which were as an enlisted soldier. Stationed at Camp Humphreys, South Korea, he serves as the Eighth Army Commanding General and United States Forces Korea (USFK) Chief of Staff.

Matthew's mother is the backbone of the family, having raised three boys while maintaining a position of unwavering support for her soldier husband, in times of both war and peace, no matter where in the world they called home.

Born in Nuremberg, Germany on September 24, 1987, that was the start of Matthew's "army brat" journey that would take him around the world, affording him opportunities most can only dream of. The army took Matthew and his family, including brothers Michael and Marc, across eight states and two countries. Growing up, Matthew was an avid snowboarder, skateboarder, and guitar player. If the ground was dry, sometimes even if it wasn't, you could find him skateboarding with his friends, many of whom he remains close with today.

Upon graduating from West Springfield High School, located in Springfield, Virginia in 2006, the fourth high school he attended in four years, Matthew attended Bellevue University in Bellevue, Nebraska. It was there that he earned a bachelor's degree in Leadership and a master's in Organizational Performance. Matthew married his high school sweetheart, Kim, in 2011.

Matthew's wife, Kim, is a success story in her own right. A MAJOR success story, to be accurate. Like Matt, Kim started her professional career while attending Bellevue University online and in the evenings. She graduated with a bachelor's degree in Business and a master's in Cyber Security. After a successful tenure at ADT Security Services and First Data, she began what would be a life-changing seven-year adventure as a Department of Defense civilian employee at United States Strategic Command, Offutt Air Force Base.

She started in the Nuclear Weapons area, and eventually transitioned to cyber security, spending her days in a windowless Sensitive Compartmented Information Facility (SCIF) called the Joint Cyber Center. In 2012, she temporarily relocated to Keesler Air Force Base for six months to attend Undergraduate Cyber Training (UCT). She was one of a very small handful of female civilians in the course designed for the air force's newest cyber officers. Upon graduating, she returned to Offutt as a cyber warrior.

Like Matthew, Kim likes to stay busy, and each night after work she began studying for her real estate license. The nature of her work both at Keesler AFB and Offutt AFB did not allow her to take work home. As a result, she knew that having her real estate license would allow her to build a business and earn extra money in her free time. What she didn't realize was just how quickly her business would take off. Fast forward to 2019, Kim left the government three years ago, she is the top agent at her firm and has done over $40 million in real estate sales to date. Almost sounds like it should be its entirely own book, doesn't it?

If there's a short list of things to take from this book, one item Matt hopes will be on that list is the importance of giving back. There really is no bigger honor in life than using one's good fortune to help another. Matt and Kim adopted a senior dachshund named Lily several years ago, and although she was only with them for eight months before passing, she had a profound impact on the two of them. She taught them about strength, perseverance, and appreciating the time we have. When they had to make the heart-wrenching decision to help her cross the rainbow bridge as a result of her failing health, they knew they would want to keep her memory alive.

Shortly after her passing, Matt and Kim created Lily's Lifeline, Inc., a non-profit organization focused on partnering with their licensed veterinarian and local animal rescue groups to provide financial assistance to animals in need of critical, but often costly, care. To date, Lily's Lifeline has contributed over $15,000 to the care of animals in need. Matt and Kim are confident Lily would be proud.

References

[1] Department of Labor, "Industries at a Glance," Bureau of Labor Statistics, 21 December 2018. [Online]. Available: https://www.bls.gov/iag/tgs/iag493.htm. [Accessed December 2018].

[2] S. Richmond, "Why Save for Retirement in Your 20's?," Investopedia, 27 September 2016. [Online]. Available: https://www.investopedia.com/articles/personal-finance/040315/why-save-retirement-your-20s.asp. [Accessed 8 October 2018].

[3] K. (. Yates, "3 in 4 Parents Help Their Adult Children with Finances," CreditCards.com, Austin, Texas, 2017.

[4] United States Department of Labor, "Employment Projections," Bureau of Labor Statistics, 2017. [Online]. Available: https://www.bls.gov/emp/chart-unemployment-earnings-education.htm. [Accessed 1 January 2019].

[5] A. Morin, "Parents, Please Don't Attend Your Adult Child's Job Interview," Forbes, 29 August 2017. [Online]. Available: https://www.forbes.com/sites/amymorin/2017/08/29/parents-please-dont-attend-your-adult-childs-job-interview/#1a938cf22a31. [Accessed 30 October 2018].

[6] M. Shean, "Here's Why You Must Teach Your Kids It's Okay to Fail," Science Alert, 10 July 2018. [Online]. Available: https://www.sciencealert.com/parenting-tips-failure-teaches-children-natural-consequence. [Accessed 1 September 2018].

[7] K. Elkins, "Here's How Much Money Americans Have in Their Savings Accounts," CNBC, 13 September 2017. [Online]. Available: https://www.cnbc.com/2017/09/13/how-much-americans-at-have-in-their-savings-accounts.html. [Accessed 2 September 2018].

[8] H. Rounds, "Average Credit Card Debt in the U.S. in 2018," Magnify Money by Lending Tree, 16 July 2018. [Online]. Available: https://www.magnifymoney.com/blog/news/u-s-credit-card-debt-by-the-numbers628618371/. [Accessed 15 November 2018].

[9] L. Boyer, "Emotional Intelligence: 10 Things You May Not Know," Leadership Options, [Online]. Available: https://lynboyer.net/emotional-intelligence-3/emotional-intelligence-10-things-you-may-not-know.html. [Accessed 29 December 2018].

[10] Anxiety and Depression Association of America, "Facts and Statistics," 2018. [Online]. Available: https://adaa.org/about-adaa/press-room/facts-statistics. [Accessed September 2018].

[11] Anxiety and Depression Association of America, "Sleep Disorders," ADAA, [Online]. Available: https://adaa.org/understanding-anxiety/related-illnesses/sleep-disorders. [Accessed 1 November 2018].

[12] K. Gander, "Millenials are the Most Anxious Generation, New Research Shows," Newsweek, 9 May 2018. [Online]. Available: https://www.newsweek.com/millennials-most-anxious-generation-new-research-shows-917095. [Accessed November 2018].

[13] Do Something.Org, "11 Facts About Anxiety," [Online]. Available: https://www.dosomething.org/us/facts/11-facts-about-anxiety. [Accessed 1 January 2019].

[14] S. Klebnikov, "8 Resourceful Ways Elon Musk Made Money Before He Was a Billionaire," Business Insider, 9 August 2017. [Online]. Available: https://www.businessinsider.com/8-resourceful-ways-elon-musk-made-money-before-he-was-a-billionaire-2017-8. [Accessed 22 December 2018].

[15] BBC News, "Elon Musk: SpaceX and Tesla alive 'by skin of their teeth'," BBC News, 11 March 2018. [Online]. Available: https://www.bbc.com/news/business-43365710. [Accessed 11 December 2018].

[16] D. Meyer, "Elon Musk Has a New Salary. He'll Only Get Paid If Tesla Shareholders Get Extremely Rich," Fortune, 23 January 2018. [Online]. Available: http://fortune.com/2018/01/23/tesla-elon-musk-targets-valuation-compensation/. [Accessed 1 January 2019].

www.ingramcontent.com/pod-product-compliance
Lightning Source LLC
Chambersburg PA
CBHW052017290426
44112CB00014B/2280